FRENCH REVOLUTION

A Cherrytree Book

Designed and produced by
A S Publishing

First published 1988
by Cherrytree Press Ltd
a subsidiary of
The Chivers Company Ltd
Windsor Bridge Road
Bath, Avon BA2 3AX
Reprinted 1989
Copyright © Cherrytree Press Ltd 1988

British Library Cataloguing in Publication Data
Hills, Ken
   French Revolution.—(Wars that changed
   the world).
   1. France—History—Revolution,
   1789-1799
   I. Title   II. McBride, Angus   III. Series
   944.04   DC149

   ISBN 0-7451-5063-2

Printed in Italy by New Interlitho, Milan

WARS THAT CHANGED THE WORLD

FRENCH REVOLUTION

By Ken Hills
Illustrated by Angus McBride *and* Tony Morris

CHERRYTREE BOOKS

The Land of France

In 1789, France seemed the foremost power in Europe. In reality, France was a land of bad government and injustice. Wars had made France poor and taxes had to be increased to pay for them. Under French law, tax was paid by those who could least afford it, the poorer people of France. The rich paid nothing.

The poor spent all they had on food to keep alive. When taxes rose, they starved. Reforms to raise more money and raise it fairly had to be made. But the reforms were not made, so in despair the poor rebelled.

In 1789, most of the 26 million people of France worked on the land. Paris was easily the largest city. About half a million people lived there.

Rich and Poor

The French nobles who owned vast estates rarely saw them. They cared little for their lands or for the people who worked on them. Land and people were used as the source of money to pay the cost of attending the king's court at Versailles. When these costs rose, the nobles merely put up the rents they collected from their tenants.

Life was always hard for the peasants who lived on their lands. When harvests were bad it was utter misery. It was not surprising that the poor acted so cruelly towards the rich when they took command during the Revolution.

English travellers in France were shocked by the hunger and poverty of the peasants. One wrote that they looked more like hungry scarecrows than people.

Paris in 1789

The city of Paris had been the capital of France for over 800 years. In 1789, more than half a million people lived there. It was easily the largest and most important city in the country. All the major decisions which affected the lives of the people were made in Paris. The important events of the Revolution took place there. The French Revolution was, more accurately, the Revolution of Paris.

Desperate for Bread

Bread was the main food of the people of Paris. Most workers spent half their wages on it. If bread ran short the price rose, and if the price rose people starved. In 1789 the price nearly doubled. Bakeries were looted by mobs of hungry citizens. They blamed the government; soon Paris was in turmoil and ripe for revolution.

The King and his Court

The king of France was the highest authority in the land. He could rule as he pleased, either in person or through officials appointed by him. He was the source of all honours, favours and appointments craved by those next in rank to him, the high French nobility. It was necessary to be near the king and to be seen by him to receive his favours, so the nobles of France, with their hundreds of relatives, servants and hangers-on, clustered around the king to form the royal court.

The king and his courtiers lived in extreme luxury. They wore gorgeous clothes and spent their time in a ceaseless round of ceremonies and entertainments. The difference between the extravagance of the court and the misery of the common people was extreme.

PARIS

The first site of Paris was the island in the River Seine now called the Île de la Cité. Paris had grown well beyond its original boundaries and the suburbs or *faubourgs* over the walls had become part of the city by the time of the Revolution.

The king lived outside his capital at Versailles, a small country town a few miles west of Paris, in the most magnificent palace in Europe.

Louis XVI stands before the palace of Versailles, built by Louis XIV. Louis XVI became king in 1774, aged 19. Louis never liked being king. Instead of discussing affairs of state with his ministers, he spent his time hunting or carving wood. In 1770 he had married Marie Antoinette, a pretty 15-year-old Austrian princess. She did not hide her reckless and extravagant way of life. She became the most hated woman in France.

Ripe for Revolution

The ordinary people who lived in cities and towns were as badly-off as the peasants who worked on the land. They were the workers in shops and factories, the street sellers, servants, and craftsmen of all kinds.

They depended entirely on their wages for living and buying food. If prices rose they went hungry, and if they lost their jobs, they starved.

Even worse off than these town workers were the hosts of unemployed people from the countryside who flocked to the bigger towns in search of work, food and shelter. Many of them survived by begging, or by robbery and violence. These were the people who formed the mobs in Paris which began the Revolution.

IN THE COUNTRY

The village had its one poor street, with its poor brewery, poor tannery, poor tavern, poor stable-yard for relays of post-horses, poor fountain, all the usual poor appointments. It had its poor people too. All its people were poor, and many of them were sitting at their doors, shredding spare onions and the like for supper, while many were at the fountain, washing leaves, and grasses, and any such small yieldings of the earth that could be eaten. Expressive signs of what made them poor, were not wanting; the tax for the state, the tax for the church, the tax for the lord, tax local and tax general, were to be paid here and to be paid there, according to solemn inscription in the little village, until the wonder was, that there was any village left unswallowed.

Charles Dickens
A Tale of Two Cities

Charles Dickens painted a vivid picture of the Revolution in his novel *A Tale of Two Cities*. This is a tiny extract from it.

Not all taxes were collected as money. Some were paid in labour. The *corvée* was a tax which forced all peasants who lived within ten miles of main roads to work on them, and keep them in good repair. They also had to repair carriage wheels.

First Estate
Second Estate
Third Estate

Members of the First and Second Estates made up only about 500,000 of France's 26 million population (top), but between them sent almost as many members to the States General as the Third Estate. They also owned about 75 per cent of the land.

The Three Estates

The French people were divided by law into three groups, called Estates. The First Estate was the clergy. The Second Estate was the nobility. There were about half a million people in these first two Estates. The rest of the country, over 25 million people, made up the Third Estate. The system dated from medieval times.

When commanded by the king, each Estate elected members from all over the country to represent it. The representatives met near the king's palace at Versailles at an assembly called the States, or Estates, General. So rare was it for kings to consult their people, that a meeting had not been called for 175 years.

The States General

Now the king was desperate. After a century of extravagance the government could not find the money to run the country or pay its debts. They had attempted to raise more money by increasing taxes but they could not raise enough. The clergy and nobility refused to be taxed. Several harvests failed and there was a shortage of bread. Food riots broke out all over the country. France was ungovernable. King Louis called the States General together to air their grievances and help him solve the country's problems. They met on 5 May 1789, but by then it was too late. The poor had run out of patience.

From the first it was clear that Louis and his ministers would not listen to the complaints of the Third Estate. Its representatives were treated like servants. They all had to dress in black and doff their hats to the nobles and clergy. They were not even allowed to use the main entrance to the assembly building, but had to come in by a side door.

THE FIRST ESTATE

The bishops and priests of the Catholic Church formed the First Estate. The Church was immensely wealthy. It owned a tenth of the land and decided how much tax to pay. The clergy had many privileges. They could not be called up for military service; they had their own courts of law and they paid few taxes. Nearly all the bishops were noblemen by birth and lived lives of great luxury. The parish priests were poor and many toiled in the fields, like the members of their congregations.

THE SECOND ESTATE

The nobles of France made up the Second Estate. They varied from royal princes to poor men who worked on their own land. Rich or poor, they had special privileges, from the right to wear a sword to exemption from certain taxes. In 1789 less than two per cent of the population were noble, yet they owned over a quarter of the land. Some titles were inherited. The king awarded the rest, sometimes in return for money, but most often through appointment to a job that carried a title with it.

THE THIRD ESTATE

The Third Estate consisted of everyone who was neither clergy nor nobility. Over 95 per cent of the French people were members of it. At the top was a small middle class of well-off tradesmen, and professionals such as lawyers and doctors. The rest, most of the people of France, varied from poor to very poor and lived as peasants in the country or as workers in the town. Whatever their position, members of the Third Estate had no privileges and no freedom from paying taxes.

11

The Revolt Begins

The Comte de Mirabeau (above) was a powerful orator and leader. When the king ordered the National Assembly to disperse, he defied him, saying, 'You will have to use bayonets to make us go.'

The storming of the Bastille (far right) on 14 July is celebrated each year as a national holiday in France.

The voting system of the States General meant that unless one of the other Estates sided with the Third Estate they could achieve nothing. Most of the clergy and nobility supported the king, so they combined to outvote the Third Estate. The Third Estate therefore resolved to meet separately from the others.

The king prevented them from using their usual meeting place, so they gathered in a nearby Royal Tennis Court on 20 June. They declared themselves the National Assembly and swore an oath to stay together until they had changed the way France was governed. The king ordered them to leave, but they refused. Weakly, he gave in and agreed to create a new assembly. In it, the Third Estate would have a clear majority.

It was a great victory for the people, but celebrations in Paris ceased when news came that royal troops were on the move against them. The Parisians got ready to fight. Early on 14 July, a vast crowd made off with 30,000 muskets from the royal armoury, and then stormed on to the Bastille prison to seize ammunition stored there.

Storming the Bastille

The Bastille was a royal fortress. There, for centuries, the French kings had shut up men without trial. It was no longer used in this way, but to the ordinary people the Bastille represented royal oppression and injustice.

The mob surrounded the Bastille and shouted to the defenders to let them in. A gun went off, and a full scale battle followed. After three hours the governor had had enough and unlocked the gates. The excited crowd rushed in and took the ammunition. The Bastille was theirs.

Inquisitive minds.
Disruptive technology.
Endless opportunity.

dyson

Enterprise started life as a small business. Still family-owned, it's grown to be the largest global mobility provider in the world, with 10,000+ branches globally, an annual turnover of $24 billion and the biggest rental vehicle fleet on the planet. Join them and be one of the people driving this success.

From their senior leaders to their apprentices, Enterprise gives everyone the freedom to explore their potential, and the opportunities they need to rise to new challenges and take their skills to the next level - because their growth is what makes Enterprise's growth possible.

Nowhere is this philosophy better illustrated than in their approach to graduate careers. When people join their award-winning Management Training Programme, they empower them to start contributing right from the word go. It helps that they are divided up into smaller, local branches, so their graduates gain the skills and experience needed to run their own business in as little as two years.

As a *Times Top 50 Employer for Women* for 15 years running, Enterprise has created a work environment where women thrive and are encouraged to rise to new levels in their career, thanks to support of both management and their peers.

Enterprise is also still family-owned – their CEO Chrissy Taylor is the third generation of the Taylor family to run the company. This allows them to look forward even more confidently to the future, providing the stability they need to pursue the long-term good for their customers, their business and their employees, even in these challenging times. Join Enterprise on their Graduate Programme, and become one of the new generation helping them write the next chapter of their success story.

GRADUATE VACANCIES IN 2021
GENERAL MANAGEMENT
RETAILING
SALES

NUMBER OF VACANCIES
450+ graduate jobs

LOCATIONS OF VACANCIES

STARTING SALARY FOR 2021
£21,000
Plus performance-based bonuses once the graduate programme has been completed, and location allowance if applicable.

UNIVERSITY PROMOTIONS DURING 2020-2021
ABERDEEN, ABERYSTWYTH, ASTON, BELFAST, BIRMINGHAM, BRADFORD, BRISTOL, BRUNEL, CARDIFF, DUNDEE, ESSEX, EXETER, GLASGOW, HERIOT-WATT, HULL, KEELE, KENT, LANCASTER, LEEDS, LEICESTER, LIVERPOOL, LOUGHBOROUGH, MANCHESTER, NEWCASTLE, NORTHUMBRIA, NOTTINGHAM, NOTTINGHAM TRENT, OXFORD BROOKES, PLYMOUTH, READING, ROYAL HOLLOWAY, SHEFFIELD, SOUTHAMPTON, STIRLING, STRATHCLYDE, SURREY, SUSSEX, SWANSEA, UEA, ULSTER, YORK
Please check with your university careers service for full details of Enterprise Rent-A-Car's local promotions and events.

APPLICATION DEADLINE
Year-round recruitment

FURTHER INFORMATION
www.Top100GraduateEmployers.com
Register now for the latest news, local promotions, work experience and vacancies at Enterprise Rent-A-Car.

Your prospects

Do wonders for them as an
Intern or **Management Trainee**

What does a graduate career with the world's largest car rental company look like? It starts in one of our 10,000 branches worldwide. It continues with you becoming a manager of one of those branches, in as little as two years' time. From there, you can go in whatever direction you choose. National sales? Business rental? Human resources? International opportunities? The choice is yours. And whether you join us on our award-winning Management Trainee program or as an Intern, you'll enjoy great benefits, excellent training and real responsibility from day one.

Discover more at
careers.enterprise.co.uk

ExxonMobil

Imagine working for one of the world's largest publicly traded energy companies, on tasks that affect nearly everyone in the world today and for future generations to come. ExxonMobil in the UK is better known for its Esso and Mobil brands due to the success of its service stations and high performance lubricants.

There's no such thing as an average day at ExxonMobil and there are many different career paths available: from a technical career to a leadership position to a commercial role. Their Engineering graduates help to create the innovative energy solutions of tomorrow, their Commercial and Business recruits focus on developing commercial opportunities, and their HR team drives competitive advantage through the company's greatest resource: its people.

For graduates who are looking for a career that will be challenging, rewarding and certainly varied, then a career with ExxonMobil might just be for them.

In addition to the competitive base salary and relocation allowance, employees are also offered a matched 2-for-1 share scheme, final salary pension plan, private health care scheme, 33 days holiday per annum (including public holidays), interest-free loan, tailored graduate training and continuous development, support towards studying for professional qualifications such as IChemE, free sports facilities and subsidised dining facilities at most locations, voluntary community activities, international opportunities and regular job rotations (typically every one to three years) with opportunities to develop and hone skills.

ExxonMobil also provides summer placements, offering first-hand experience to learn how a leading engineering organisation works. Students are asked to work in groups on real company projects, interacting with people from a variety of disciplines and levels of the organisation.

GRADUATE VACANCIES IN 2021
ENGINEERING
HUMAN RESOURCES
MARKETING

NUMBER OF VACANCIES
No fixed quota

LOCATIONS OF VACANCIES

STARTING SALARY FOR 2021
£Competitive

UNIVERSITY PROMOTIONS DURING 2020-2021
Please check with your university careers service for full details of ExxonMobil's local promotions and events.

MINIMUM ENTRY REQUIREMENTS
2.1 Degree

APPLICATION DEADLINE
Varies by function

FURTHER INFORMATION
www.Top100GraduateEmployers.com
Register now for the latest news, local promotions, work experience and graduate vacancies at ExxonMobil.

EY
Building a better
working world

EY is one of the world's most influential professional services organisations. Operating across 150 countries, EY has built a reputation as a trusted partner to its clients, helping them to make better business, technology and finance decisions. How? By asking better questions that inspire a better working world.

With 300,000 people working within four key business areas – Assurance, Consulting, Strategy and Transactions, and Tax – EY is well-equipped to deliver sustainable and inclusive solutions that meet a variety of client challenges. By asking these clients better questions, the company puts a focus on continuous improvement, not just within this one industry, but across entire economies and societies, transforming the way businesses work.

This transformative culture allows EY to offer each colleague the opportunity to do truly impactful work. To help companies big and small, global and local, navigate the ever-changing world. Whatever their role, whichever business area they choose, colleagues across the UK are given the chance to craft their own extraordinary experiences. Experiences that will propel them into the future. Experiences that will help them reinvent the working world.

What does this mean for students? At EY, each student and graduate gets to work on real client projects, helping to bring strategies to life, innovate new initiatives and activate EY's purpose. This is a business that takes student opportunities and turns them into lifelong career journeys. So, for students who are curious, adaptable, resilient and collaborative, one of EY's programmes could be the perfect match. Somewhere they can add long-term value to communities and organisations the world over. Somewhere they can form long-lasting, meaningful networks. Somewhere they can truly belong. It's their project. It's theirs to build.

GRADUATE VACANCIES IN 2021

ACCOUNTANCY

CONSULTING

FINANCE

TECHNOLOGY

NUMBER OF VACANCIES
700-800 graduate jobs

LOCATIONS OF VACANCIES

STARTING SALARY FOR 2021
£Competitive

**UNIVERSITY PROMOTIONS
DURING 2020-2021**
ABERDEEN, ASTON, BELFAST, BIRMINGHAM, BRISTOL, CAMBRIDGE, CARDIFF, DUNDEE, DURHAM, EDINBURGH, EXETER, GLASGOW, HERIOT-WATT, HULL, KING'S COLLEGE LONDON, LANCASTER, LEEDS, LEICESTER, LIVERPOOL, LONDON SCHOOL OF ECONOMICS, MANCHESTER, NEWCASTLE, NORTHUMBRIA, NOTTINGHAM, QUEEN MARY LONDON, READING, SHEFFIELD, SOUTHAMPTON, ST ANDREWS, STIRLING, STRATHCLYDE, SURREY, UEA, UNIVERSITY COLLEGE LONDON, WARWICK, YORK
Please check with your university careers service for full details of EY's local promotions and events.

APPLICATION DEADLINE
Year-round recruitment
Early application advised.

FURTHER INFORMATION
www.Top100GraduateEmployers.com
Register now for the latest news, local promotions, work experience and graduate vacancies at EY.

FRONTLINE

CHANGING LIVES

thefrontline.org.uk

facebook.com/FrontlineChangingLives **f**

recruitment@thefrontline.org.uk ✉

linkedin.com/company/frontline-org **in**

twitter.com/FrontlineSW 𝕏

instagram.com/Frontline_SW 📷

youtube.com/FrontlineChangingLives ▶

Frontline recruits and develops outstanding individuals to be social workers. No child's life chances should be limited by their social or family circumstances. Frontline's mission is to create social change for children who do not have a safe or stable home, by developing excellent social work practice and leadership.

Social workers support some of the most disadvantaged children and families in the community. On Frontline's two-year graduate programme, participants will have a vital impact in their local community from almost day one and make a real, positive difference to society through their work. They will also gain skills in leadership, conflict resolution and relationship building to thrive in this dynamic and challenging role.

The programme kicks off with five weeks of intensive residential training, where participants will learn the foundational skills and knowledge required for direct work with children and families in their community. They then start a two-year placement in a local authority children's services team, honing and developing these skills on the job.

Working in a close-knit unit with other Frontline programme participants and an experienced leader, participants will discuss ideas, connect theory to practice, and have space for self-reflection; all of which enhances their learning experience. Participants receive high-quality supervision from experienced social workers, academics and professional leadership coaches, giving them tailored support to develop their skills for social work and beyond.

During the programme, participants qualify as a social work professional through a fully-funded Master's degree whilst also getting a tax free £18,000-£20,000 bursary in year one and earning up to £34,000 in year two.

Join Frontline and work to deliver social change for children and families.

GRADUATE VACANCIES IN 2021
SOCIAL WORK

NUMBER OF VACANCIES
452 graduate jobs

LOCATIONS OF VACANCIES

STARTING SALARY FOR 2021
£18,000-£20,000
As a bursary.

UNIVERSITY PROMOTIONS DURING 2020-2021
BIRMINGHAM, BRISTOL, CAMBRIDGE, CARDIFF, DURHAM, EDINBURGH, EXETER, KING'S COLLEGE LONDON, KENT, LANCASTER, LEEDS, LEICESTER, LIVERPOOL, LONDON SCHOOL OF ECONOMICS, LOUGHBOROUGH, MANCHESTER, NEWCASTLE, NOTTINGHAM, NOTTINGHAM TRENT, OXFORD, SHEFFIELD, UNIVERSITY COLLEGE LONDON, WARWICK, YORK
Please check with your university careers service for full details of Frontline's local promotions and events.

MINIMUM ENTRY REQUIREMENTS
2.1 Degree

APPLICATION DEADLINE
Year-round recruitment
Early application advised.

FURTHER INFORMATION
www.Top100GraduateEmployers.com
Register now for the latest news, local promotions, work experience and graduate vacancies at Frontline.

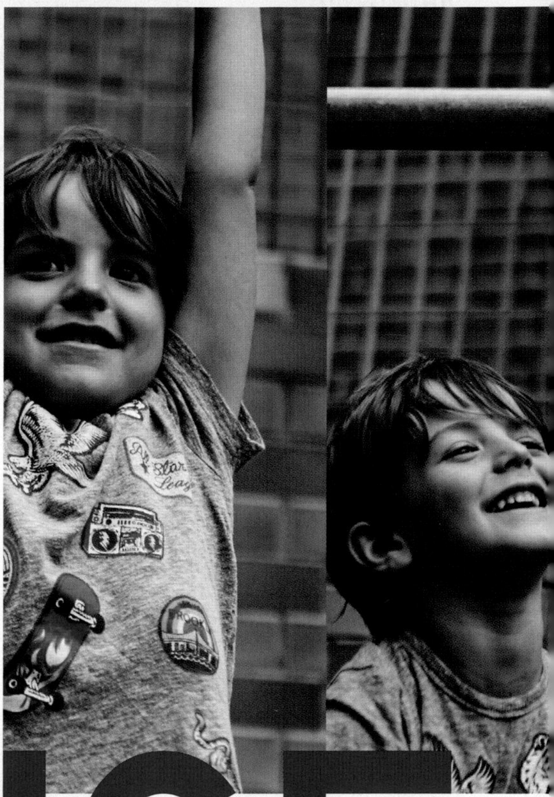

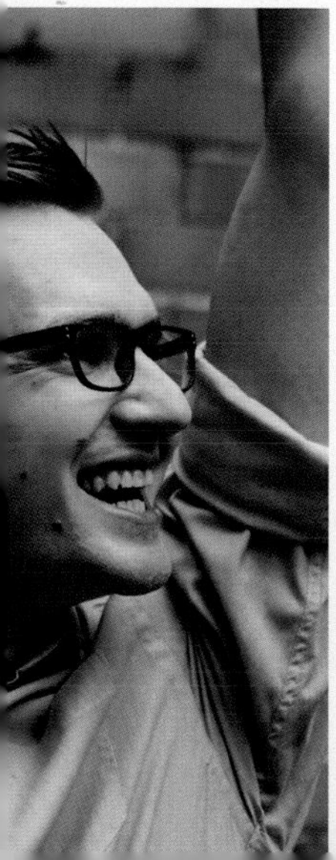

Government Communications Headquarters (GCHQ) is the UK's signals intelligence and cyber security agency. It works alongside MI5 and SIS (MI6) to keep the UK and its citizens safe at home, overseas and online. Using cutting-edge technology and technical ingenuity, GCHQ's mission is to counter threats including terrorism, espionage, organised crime and cyber-attacks.

GCHQ is looking for graduates with different skills, backgrounds and perspectives to help protect the UK. There are a range of graduate roles available in areas including technology, maths, language, and analysis, as well as in corporate roles including finance, project management, and procurement. Students can take advantage of a variety of paid summer placements. Bursaries are also available to students studying any degree who have an interest in cyber security. Graduates joining GCHQ can expect challenging projects, outstanding professional development and a rewarding career experience.

GCHQ is proud of its mission and its people. Its working culture encourages open minds and attitudes and is supported by a welfare and benefits structure that enables its workforce to be at its best. From extensive training and development that helps employees expand their skills, to flexible working patterns that support a healthy work-life balance, GCHQ seeks to create an environment where everyone can achieve their full potential.

Applications are welcome from everyone, regardless of age, experience, cultural background and sexual orientation. Due to the sensitive nature of the work, there are strict nationality, residency and security requirements and all applicants will be subject to a rigorous but fair vetting process. Applicants will need to be British citizens and need to have lived in the UK for seven out of the last ten years before applying, although some exceptions may apply.

GRADUATE VACANCIES IN 2021
ENGINEERING
GENERAL MANAGEMENT
RESEARCH & DEVELOPMENT
TECHNOLOGY

NUMBER OF VACANCIES
50+ graduate jobs

LOCATIONS OF VACANCIES

STARTING SALARY FOR 2021
£30,000

UNIVERSITY PROMOTIONS DURING 2020-2021
Please check with your university careers service for full details of GCHQ's local promotions and events.

APPLICATION DEADLINE
Varies by function

FURTHER INFORMATION
www.Top100GraduateEmployers.com
Register now for the latest news, local promotions, work experience and graduate vacancies at GCHQ.

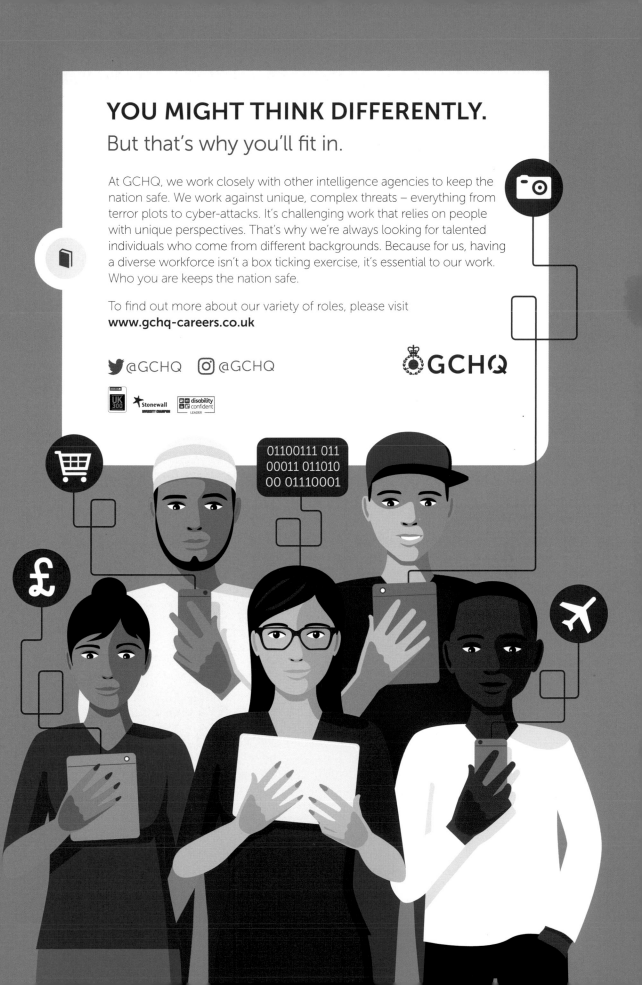

Goldman Sachs is a leading global financial services firm providing investment banking, securities and investment management services to a substantial and diversified client base that includes corporations, financial institutions, governments and individuals.

Goldman Sachs seeks out people with all types of skills, interests and experiences. There's no template for the "right" Goldman Sachs employee, which is why they search for talent in new places and in new ways, seeking different majors, personalities, experiences, skills and working styles.

For them, it's all about bringing together people who are curious, collaborative and have the drive to make things possible for their clients and communities.

With 70+ offices and 36,000+ people, Goldman Sachs is constantly evolving and innovating to shape the future of finance and help its clients in an ever-changing world.

The Goldman Sachs culture fosters an environment that enables colleagues to fulfil their highest aspirations, both professionally and personally. From digital learning and leadership development training to resilience and mindfulness offerings, they are invested in all aspects of their workforce and are committed to growth at every level.

At Goldman Sachs, their goal is to attract the extraordinarily talented and diverse people needed to drive their business into the future. Diversity and inclusion is a business imperative and they strive to cultivate a work experience where its people can reach their full potential and thrive as their authentic selves. For Goldman Sachs' people to excel, everyone must feel that they are operating in an inclusive environment that celebrates differences and values different ways of thinking.

GRADUATE VACANCIES IN 2021
ACCOUNTANCY
ENGINEERING
FINANCE
HUMAN RESOURCES
INVESTMENT BANKING
LAW
RESEARCH & DEVELOPMENT
SALES
TECHNOLOGY

NUMBER OF VACANCIES
400 graduate jobs

LOCATIONS OF VACANCIES

Vacancies also available in Europe, the USA, Asia, and elsewhere in the world.

STARTING SALARY FOR 2021
£Competitive
Plus a competitive bonus and relocation allowance.

UNIVERSITY PROMOTIONS DURING 2020-2021
Please check with your university careers service for full details of Goldman Sachs' local promotions and events.

APPLICATION DEADLINE
22nd November 2020

FURTHER INFORMATION
www.Top100GraduateEmployers.com
*Register now for the latest news, local promotions, work experience and graduate vacancies at **Goldman Sachs**.*

Curious, collaborative and driven? Let's chat.

See yourself here.

At Goldman Sachs, we believe who you are makes you better at what you do. We seek out people with all types of skills, interests and experiences. Even if you have never imagined a career in finance, there's a place for you here. For us, it's all about bringing together people who are curious, collaborative and have the drive to make things possible for our clients and communities.

Interested? We'd love to meet you – join us at our upcoming events or programmes to meet us and learn more about the opportunities we offer.

EMEA APPLICATION DEADLINES

We review applications on a rolling basis and encourage you to apply as soon as you are ready.

22 November 2020
- New Analyst Programme (ex Engineering / Warsaw)
- Summer Analyst Programme (ex Engineering / Warsaw)
- Spring Programme
- Work Placement Programme

31 January 2021
- Engineering New Analyst
- Engineering Summer Analyst

Rolling Deadlines
- Rolling Deadlines
- Warsaw (All Programmes)
- EMEA Off-Cycle Programmes

Make things possible.

google.com/students

facebook.com/GoogleStudents
linkedin.com/company/google   twitter.com/GoogleStudents
instagram.com/GoogleStudents   youtube.com/GoogleStudents

GRADUATE VACANCIES IN 2021

CONSULTING
ENGINEERING
HUMAN RESOURCES
MARKETING
SALES
TECHNOLOGY

NUMBER OF VACANCIES
No fixed quota

LOCATIONS OF VACANCIES

Vacancies also available in Europe.

STARTING SALARY FOR 2021
£Competitive

UNIVERSITY PROMOTIONS DURING 2020-2021
Please check with your university careers service for full details of Google's local promotions and events.

MINIMUM ENTRY REQUIREMENTS
Relevant degree required for some roles.

APPLICATION DEADLINE
Year-round recruitment

FURTHER INFORMATION
www.Top100GraduateEmployers.com
Register now for the latest news, local promotions, work experience and graduate vacancies at Google.

Larry Page and Sergey Brin founded Google in September 1998 with a mission to organise the world's information and make it universally accessible and useful. Since then, the company has grown to more than 120,000 employees worldwide, with a wide range of popular products and platforms.

A problem isn't truly solved until it's solved for all.

Googlers build products that help create opportunities for everyone, whether down the street or across the globe. They bring insight, imagination, and a healthy disregard for the impossible. They bring everything that makes them unique. It's really the people that make Google the kind of company it is. Google hires people who are smart and determined, and favours their ability over their experience.

Google hires graduates from all disciplines, from humanities and business related courses to engineering and computer science. The ideal candidate is someone who can demonstrate a passion for the online industry and someone who has made the most of their time at university through involvement in clubs, societies or relevant internships. Google hires graduates who have a variety of strengths and passions, not just isolated skill sets. For technical roles within engineering teams, specific skills will be required. The diversity of perspectives, ideas, and cultures, both within Google and in the tech industry overall, leads to the creation of better products and services.

Whether it's providing online marketing consultancy, selling an advertising solution to clients, hiring the next generation of Googlers, or building products, Google has full-time roles and internships available across teams like global customer solutions, sales, people operations, legal, finance, operations, cloud and engineering.

Build
for
everyone

Together, we can
create opportunities
for people to learn, be
heard, and succeed.
google.com/students

Google

facebook.com/GrantThorntonRecruitmentUK   traineerecruitment@uk.gt.com

linkedin.com/company/grant-thornton-uk-llp   twitter.com/GT_STB

instagram.com/GT_trainees   youtube.com/GTSpillingTheBeans

Grant Thornton

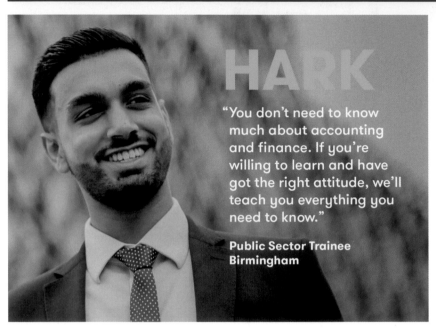

HARK

"You don't need to know much about accounting and finance. If you're willing to learn and have got the right attitude, we'll teach you everything you need to know."

**Public Sector Trainee
Birmingham**

Grant Thornton is one of the world's leading independent assurance, tax and advisory firms. They are driven by independent thinkers that provide high quality business and financial advice to a wide range of clients in countries all over the world. Shape more than just your career at Grant Thornton.

In Grant Thornton's graduate programme, graduates get the training and support to help them grow in confidence and to develop the skills they need to become a future leader. But they'll also do so much more than that. With a relentless focus on quality and integrity, graduates will help businesses to achieve their objectives and flourish.

Graduates join a three-year programme to become professionally qualified advisers, specialising in either advisory, audit or tax. In this training programme, they'll get hands-on experience working with clients, from multinationals to start-ups, across public and private sectors.

Grant Thornton's graduate programme is just the beginning. Once graduates get their qualification, all kinds of career routes will open up to them, from audit, tax and advisory to people management and business development. What happens next and how fast they progress is up to them. Grant Thornton has a flexible approach to academic entry requirements. The firm will consider applicants' academic achievements, but their strengths, motivations and connection with the business and its values are more important.

They are looking for people with a broad range of interests and experiences. Grant Thornton does things differently. They give their people the freedom to drive change and shape their own destinies. Their people are inspired to make a difference. Their collaborative culture means they share ideas as well as the responsibility for making them happen.

GRADUATE VACANCIES IN 2021
ACCOUNTANCY

NUMBER OF VACANCIES
300-350 graduate jobs

LOCATIONS OF VACANCIES

STARTING SALARY FOR 2021
£Competitive

UNIVERSITY PROMOTIONS DURING 2020-2021
ASTON, BATH, BIRMINGHAM, BRISTOL, CAMBRIDGE, CARDIFF, CITY, DURHAM, EDINBURGH, EXETER, GLASGOW, HERIOT-WATT, KING'S COLLEGE LONDON, KENT, LEEDS, LEICESTER, LIVERPOOL, LOUGHBOROUGH, MANCHESTER, NEWCASTLE, NOTTINGHAM, NOTTINGHAM TRENT, OXFORD BROOKES, QUEEN MARY LONDON, READING, SHEFFIELD, SOUTHAMPTON, STIRLING, STRATHCLYDE, SURREY, UNIVERSITY COLLEGE LONDON, YORK
Please check with your university careers service for full details of Grant Thornton's local promotions and events.

APPLICATION DEADLINE
Year-round recruitment
Early application advised.

FURTHER INFORMATION
www.Top100GraduateEmployers.com
Register now for the latest news, local promotions, work experience and graduate vacancies at Grant Thornton.

SHAPE MORE THAN JUST YOUR CAREER

At Grant Thornton we have a unique culture where thinking differently is encouraged, your opinions are heard and your contributions are valued. Our people are given the freedom to drive change and shape their own destinies. So if you'd like to make a difference, bring your passion, ambitions and inspiration, and together let's make it happen.

trainees.grantthornton.co.uk

Grant Thornton
An instinct for growth™

gsk.com/en-gb/careers/future-leaders

facebook.com/GSKcareers
linkedin.com/company/glaxosmithkline twitter.com/GSK
instagram.com/GSK youtube.com/GSK

GSK has a challenging and inspiring mission: to improve the quality of human life by enabling people to do more, feel better and live longer. As one of the world's leading healthcare companies, GSK discovers, develops and manufactures medicines, vaccines and consumer products.

The chance to help millions of people do more, feel better and live longer? The opportunity to launch a graduate career in a responsive, innovative, global business? An undergraduate placement that will provide practical experience? A company that's genuinely committed to personal and professional growth? GSK has the answers.

Graduates can join the company in a variety of exciting roles across a wide range of business functions. GSK needs future scientists to discover, future engineers and supply chain managers to deliver, future commercial teams to understand patients and consumers, and they need tomorrow's experts in IT, finance, HR, communications and procurement to achieve outstanding business performance.

The company's Future Leaders get an unparalleled insight into the enormous depth, breadth and influence of the business. GSK are deeply committed to personal and professional development – offering a range of ongoing and tailored learning opportunities. GSK give their people the trust and respect to be themselves, and the chance to develop their careers across an incredibly diverse collection of businesses and geographies.

Successful candidates will flourish in an environment where personal growth plays a vital part in the changing face of the business. But most of all, graduates will enjoy the sense of purpose that comes from leading change in an industry that touches millions every day.

GRADUATE VACANCIES IN 2021
ENGINEERING
FINANCE
HUMAN RESOURCES
LOGISTICS
MARKETING
PURCHASING
RESEARCH & DEVELOPMENT
SALES
TECHNOLOGY

NUMBER OF VACANCIES
50+ graduate jobs

LOCATIONS OF VACANCIES

STARTING SALARY FOR 2021
£30,000+
Plus bonus.

UNIVERSITY PROMOTIONS DURING 2020-2021
ASTON, BATH, BIRMINGHAM, BRADFORD, BRUNEL, CITY, HULL, IMPERIAL COLLEGE LONDON, KING'S COLLEGE LONDON, KENT, LANCASTER, LEEDS, LEICESTER, LIVERPOOL, LOUGHBOROUGH, MANCHESTER, NEWCASTLE, NORTHUMBRIA, NOTTINGHAM, NOTTINGHAM TRENT, QUEEN MARY LONDON, SHEFFIELD, STRATHCLYDE, SURREY, UNIVERSITY COLLEGE LONDON, YORK
Please check with your university careers service for full details of GSK's local promotions and events.

APPLICATION DEADLINE
Varies by function

FURTHER INFORMATION
www.Top100GraduateEmployers.com
Register now for the latest news, local promotions, work experience and graduate vacancies at GSK.

Open discovery

Join our Future Leaders programme

Want to help tackle some of the world's biggest healthcare challenges? We're a global company delivering billions of innovative products every year, helping boost the health of hundreds of millions worldwide. Join us and whatever role you're in – from scientific research to engineering, from sales to finance – you'll help people do more, feel better, live longer.

Discover more at
gsk.com/careers

Herbert Smith Freehills is a leading, full-service international law firm that works on some of the most important cases and deals for the world's biggest organisations. As the world continues to evolve at an unprecedented pace, they are continuing to build an organisation ready for tomorrow.

Defined by their inclusive culture and commitment to innovation, Herbert Smith Freehills give trainees the platform and responsibility to make an impact from day one. They are inviting graduates to build a career, help lead them into tomorrow, and shape the industry's future.

Few operate at the forefront of so many exciting sectors, they combine legal expertise with a global perspective and local insight. With over 3,000 lawyers in 26 international offices, their leading international teams include an award-winning in-house advocacy unit and dispute resolution team, which is recognised as number one globally.

That exceptional performance is due to innovation being at the heart of everything they do. At Herbert Smith Freehills, it's less about being ready for the future and more about being ready to lead it. That means everyone is expected to bring new ideas to the work they do and how they do it. All lawyers, including graduates, harness the latest technology to drive better outcomes and have the platform to drive and deliver innovations that bring the future of law to life.

Trainees are a part of making that future happen. All trainees tailor their training contracts and sit in a broad range of practice groups, including the firm's leading corporate and disputes teams. They are given real responsibility across both fee-earning work and pro bono initiatives. Trainees get the essential combination of a global and progressive approach that provides a true insight into the future of law and a platform to shape their place in it.

GRADUATE VACANCIES IN 2021

LAW

NUMBER OF VACANCIES
60 graduate jobs
For training contracts starting in 2023.

LOCATIONS OF VACANCIES

STARTING SALARY FOR 2021
£45,000

UNIVERSITY PROMOTIONS DURING 2020-2021
BIRMINGHAM, BRISTOL, CAMBRIDGE, DURHAM, EDINBURGH, ESSEX, EXETER, GLASGOW, IMPERIAL COLLEGE LONDON, KING'S COLLEGE LONDON, KENT, LEEDS, LEICESTER, LIVERPOOL, LONDON SCHOOL OF ECONOMICS, MANCHESTER, NOTTINGHAM, OXFORD, QUEEN MARY LONDON, SHEFFIELD, SOUTHAMPTON, UEA, UNIVERSITY COLLEGE LONDON, WARWICK, YORK
Please check with your university careers service for full details of Herbert Smith Freehills' local promotions and events.

MINIMUM ENTRY REQUIREMENTS
2.1 Degree

APPLICATION DEADLINE
14th December 2020
For spring and summer vacation schemes. See website for other deadlines.

FURTHER INFORMATION
www.Top100GraduateEmployers.com
Register now for the latest news, local promotions, work experience and graduate vacancies at HSF.

HERBERT
SMITH
FREEHILLS

THE FUTURE OF
LAW IS HERE

26	14	£45K	25,856	10
OFFICES GLOBALLY	INTERNATIONAL SECONDMENTS	IN FIRST YEAR	HOURS OF PRO BONO & CSR ADVICE	DAYS FOR INNOVATION

INCLUSIVE   CHALLENGING   PROGRESSIVE   DIVERSE   INNOVATIVE

CAREERS.HERBERTSMITHFREEHILLS.COM/UK/GRADS

Hogan Lovells

graduates.hoganlovells.com

graduate.recruitment@hoganlovells.com

twitter.com/HLGraduatesUK
facebook.com/HoganLovellsGradsUK
instagram.com/HoganLovellsGradsUK
linkedin.com/company/hoganlovells

At any given moment around the world, Hogan Lovells are changing the game. With 2,600+ lawyers in 48 global offices, they're working on projects that shape legal precedent, enabling innovations for prestigious clients. The best part? They act as one team, working seamlessly across continents.

But staying ahead of the curve takes agility: the ability to innovate, embrace industry developments, and adapt in a changing world. That's why this year, there are virtual opportunities to get to know the firm, including internships, insight events, law fairs, webinars, workshops and more.

All virtual opportunities are packed with insight and practical experience. Students will meet the firm's lawyers, delve into broad practice groups and high-profile projects, develop their own commercial awareness, and learn more about the role of a trainee solicitor.

The firm's two-year training contracts focus on hands-on learning and expert guidance. Graduates develop a deep understanding of Hogan Lovells' bold and distinctive approach to creating valuable global solutions, as they learn from a diverse network of wide-ranging specialists.

Here's how it works: graduates do four six-month seats across different practice groups – Corporate and Finance, Global Regulatory and IPMT, Litigation Arbitration and Employment. Plus, for one of those seats, they'll have the chance to apply for an international or client secondment.

No matter where they come from or which path they take, graduates grow their legal expertise, sharpen their commercial edge and tackle fascinating challenges for some of the most well-respected clients across the globe. Furthermore, they'll be part of a close-knit team – with support and encouragement from everyone around them. Now that's game-changing.

GRADUATE VACANCIES IN 2021

LAW

NUMBER OF VACANCIES
Up to 50 graduate jobs
For training contracts starting in 2023.

LOCATIONS OF VACANCIES

STARTING SALARY FOR 2021
£46,000

UNIVERSITY PROMOTIONS DURING 2020-2021
BIRMINGHAM, BRISTOL, CAMBRIDGE, CARDIFF, CITY, DURHAM, EDINBURGH, EXETER, HULL, IMPERIAL COLLEGE LONDON, KING'S COLLEGE LONDON, KENT, LEEDS, LONDON SCHOOL OF ECONOMICS, MANCHESTER, NEWCASTLE, NOTTINGHAM, OXFORD, QUEEN MARY LONDON, SCHOOL OF AFRICAN STUDIES, SHEFFIELD, UEA, UNIVERSITY COLLEGE LONDON, WARWICK, YORK
Please check with your university careers service for full details of Hogan Lovells' local promotions and events.

MINIMUM ENTRY REQUIREMENTS
2.1 Degree

APPLICATION DEADLINE
Law: 31st July 2021
Non-law: 31st January 2021

FURTHER INFORMATION
www.Top100GraduateEmployers.com
*Register now for the latest news, local promotions, work experience and graduate vacancies at **Hogans Lovells**.*

HSBC

With a network of some 3,800 offices in 64 countries and territories, serving more than 40 million customers, HSBC is one of the largest most diverse global banks. HSBC's purpose is to be where the growth is, enabling businesses to thrive and economies to prosper.

HSBC is looking for new students and graduates who are collaborative and curious thinkers, with the courage to challenge the status quo and the motivation to make a positive impact for customers worldwide.

HSBC is focused on building a sustainable future and serving the needs of a changing world. It knows that economic growth must be sustainable for colleagues, customers and communities. Its approach focuses on three main areas: sustainable finance and the global transition to a low-carbon economy; sustainable supply chains; and employability and financial capability.

HSBC puts diversity at the heart of their business, and wants a connected and international workforce of unique thinkers who are open to a range of perspectives that reflect the communities and markets in which they serve.

HSBC provides an open, supportive, and inclusive working environment, providing tailored training and support to help employees thrive in their chosen career path.

No matter what interests and skills a student or graduate might have, a career at HSBC will give them the opportunities, experiences, networks and training they need – so there's no limit to how far they'll go.

Students and graduates can apply to join intern and graduate programmes across the bank in the following areas: Commercial Banking, Global Banking & Markets, Wealth and Personal Banking (including Global Asset Management and Private Banking) or HSBC Operations, Services and Technology.

GRADUATE VACANCIES IN 2021

ACCOUNTANCY
FINANCE
GENERAL MANAGEMENT
INVESTMENT BANKING
RETAILING
TECHNOLOGY

NUMBER OF VACANCIES
600+ graduate jobs

LOCATIONS OF VACANCIES

Vacancies also available in Europe, the USA, Asia and elsewhere in the world.

STARTING SALARY FOR 2021
£Competitive
Plus a competitive joining bonus.

UNIVERSITY PROMOTIONS DURING 2020-2021
ABERDEEN, ABERYSTWYTH, ASTON, BANGOR, BATH, BELFAST, BIRMINGHAM, BRADFORD, BRISTOL, BRUNEL, CAMBRIDGE, CARDIFF, CITY, TRINITY COLLEGE DUBLIN, UNIVERSITY COLLEGE DUBLIN, DUNDEE, DURHAM, EDINBURGH, ESSEX, EXETER, GLASGOW, HERIOT-WATT, HULL, IMPERIAL COLLEGE LONDON, KEELE, KING'S COLLEGE LONDON, KENT, LANCASTER, LEEDS, LEICESTER, LIVERPOOL, LONDON SCHOOL OF ECONOMICS, LOUGHBOROUGH, MANCHESTER, NEWCASTLE, NORTHUMBRIA, NOTTINGHAM, NOTTINGHAM TRENT, OXFORD, OXFORD BROOKES, PLYMOUTH, QUEEN MARY LONDON, READING, ROYAL HOLLOWAY, SCHOOL OF AFRICAN STUDIES, SHEFFIELD, SOUTHAMPTON, ST ANDREWS, STIRLING, STRATHCLYDE, SURREY, SUSSEX, SWANSEA, UEA, ULSTER, UNIVERSITY COLLEGE LONDON, WARWICK, YORK
Please check with your university careers service for full details of HSBC's local promotions and events.

MINIMUM ENTRY REQUIREMENTS
2.1 Degree
120 UCAS points
300 UCAS points for those who passed exams before 2017.

APPLICATION DEADLINE
Varies by function

FURTHER INFORMATION
www.Top100GraduateEmployers.com
Register now for the latest news, local promotions, work experience and graduate vacancies at HSBC.

You want to make an impact

u're interested in
coming a part of our
obal community. We'll
nnect you with our
verse network, all working
wards a common goal.
d we'll help you embrace
e possibilities and shared
periences of learning.

We'll give you a world of support to do it

As you grow, we grow.
Discover intern and graduate opportunities
at hsbc.com/earlycareers

IBM is one of the world's largest technology and consulting firms. However, at IBM, work is more than a job - it's a calling: To build. To design. To code. To consult. To make markets. To invent. To collaborate. Not just to do something better, but to attempt things that people never thought possible.

IBM's graduate scheme will give graduates everything they need to build the kind of career they want. With graduate salaries starting at £32,000, a flexible benefits package and opportunities in consulting, technology and design, they will work on challenging projects, have real responsibility, and have access to world class opportunities. They'll be able to collaborate with people who are open-minded and excited about the same things they are.

IBM are looking for enthusiastic, driven and innovative individuals from any degree background. For the company's graduate schemes, applicants will have needed to achieve a 2:1 or higher in any degree discipline. IBM's most successful graduates share a distinct set of characteristics. These begin with energy and creativity, along with a clear focus on delivering exceptional customer service. IBM look for eight specific competencies during the application process: adaptability, communication, client focus, creative problem solving, teamwork, passion for IBM and taking ownership. If potential applicants love working with people and they thrive in a collaborative culture, then they'll fit right in.

Skills development is key to an IBMer's success. To further enhance their Professional Development, there are opportunities for coaching and mentoring, and these graduates will even get a dedicated manager. They will then have the opportunity to apply their knowledge in a commercial environment, via 'on-the-job training', adding value to IBM and its clients.

GRADUATE VACANCIES IN 2021
CONSULTING
TECHNOLOGY

NUMBER OF VACANCIES
150+ graduate jobs

LOCATIONS OF VACANCIES

STARTING SALARY FOR 2021
£32,000

UNIVERSITY PROMOTIONS DURING 2020-2021
ABERYSTWYTH, ASTON, BATH, BIRMINGHAM, BRADFORD, BRISTOL, BRUNEL, CARDIFF, DURHAM, EXETER, IMPERIAL COLLEGE LONDON, KING'S COLLEGE LONDON, LEEDS, LEICESTER, LIVERPOOL, LOUGHBOROUGH, MANCHESTER, NOTTINGHAM, NOTTINGHAM TRENT, OXFORD, OXFORD BROOKES, READING, SOUTHAMPTON, UNIVERSITY COLLEGE LONDON, WARWICK
Please check with your university careers service for full details of IBM's local promotions and events.

MINIMUM ENTRY REQUIREMENTS
2.1 Degree

APPLICATION DEADLINE
Varies by function

FURTHER INFORMATION
www.Top100GraduateEmployers.com
Register now for the latest news, local promotions, work experience and graduate vacancies at IBM.

IBM Let's put smart to work.™

Do your best work ever.

What can you do at IBM?

Our Graduate schemes will give you everything you need to build the career you want. You will work on challenging projects, have real responsibility and have access to world class opportunities. With the support of 380,000 collegues worldwide, you'll gain the experience, skills and contacts you need to help us solve some of our client's toughest challenges.

ibm.com/jobs/uk

Bianca
Joined 2008

 IBMCareersUKI

IBMCareersUKI

jaguarlandrovercareers.com

twitter.com/JLRcareers   facebook.com/JLRearlycareers **f**

instagram.com/JLRcareers   linkedin.com/company/jaguar-land-rover_1

A tech-driven revolution is transforming the industry, and Jaguar Land Rover are on a journey to lead that transformation: a journey that requires people who can see the opportunity in a challenge. So, finding the next generation of innovators – bright and passionate people – is crucial.

Jaguar Land Rover is a British technology company with a global reach. They are harnessing technology to make driving smarter, safer and cleaner. Graduates can help create a world in which responsible, sustainable vehicles revolutionise the driving experience for generations.

New recruits need a creative and commercially focused approach to their work. Bring that, and Jaguar Land Rover has all the opportunities and rewards to help graduates learn, develop and apply their skills. The graduate scheme has been designed to be as inspiring as the vehicles that successful applicants will help to design, engineer and sell. As one of the UK's largest investors in research and innovation, education is a critical part of Jaguar Land Rover's business strategy and ambition. It aims to hire the best talent and, then, through lifelong learning, aims to enable them to learn, create, grow and to support others to do the same. These opportunities range across the business, from engineering, manufacturing and software design to commercial and business areas.

As would be expected from two of the world's most revered brands, a range of rewards and benefits await those who have the initiative, vision and drive to contribute to the organisation's global success – including a competitive salary, joining bonus, pension scheme and discount car purchase scheme. There is also the opportunity to study for a chartered qualification as part of the programme.

All this, and more, makes Jaguar Land Rover an enviable place for graduates to start their journey.

GRADUATE VACANCIES IN 2021

ENGINEERING

LOGISTICS

RESEARCH & DEVELOPMENT

TECHNOLOGY

NUMBER OF VACANCIES
50-100 graduate jobs

LOCATIONS OF VACANCIES

STARTING SALARY FOR 2021
£29,000
Plus a £2,000 joining bonus.

UNIVERSITY PROMOTIONS DURING 2020-2021
Please check with your university careers service for full details of Jaguar Land Rover's local promotions and events.

MINIMUM ENTRY REQUIREMENTS
2.2 Degree

FURTHER INFORMATION
www.Top100GraduateEmployers.com
*Register now for the latest news, local promotions, work experience and graduate vacancies at **Jaguar Land Rover**.*

CHANGING THE WAY
THE WORLD MOVES

WHAT PART WILL YOU PLAY?

Changing the way the world moves means delivering experiences
people love, for life. And everyone plays their part in delivering or
blueprint for success You could be starting a lifelong journey of
innovation and discovery. Of excitement and adventure.

Visit jaguarlandrovercareers.com

THINK BEYOND

KPMG

With a worldwide presence, KPMG continues to build on its member firms' successes thanks to a clear vision, its people and its Values. This year celebrates 150 years of KPMG in the UK supporting businesses to grow, its people to achieve and its communities to thrive.

Its largest practice is Audit, which helps to build the confidence and trust that business and society needs. In Tax, KPMG Law, Consulting, Deal Advisory and Technology & Engineering, KPMG helps companies to solve some of their most complex business challenges.

Like the organisations they work with, KPMG is embracing change with new ways of working and innovative technology unlocking opportunity in a digitally-driven age. Trainees have access to advanced technologies, such as artificial intelligence and the latest Cloud tools. KPMG Clara – the firm's progressive global collaboration and analytics tool – enables their audit teams to provide quality insights and consistency across all audit engagements.

KPMG colleagues come from all sorts of degree disciplines and backgrounds bringing diverse perspectives, whilst sharing a natural curiosity, a digital mindset and a desire to work together, explore new ideas and deliver exceptional results.

In return for all their hard work, graduates will benefit from funded, relevant professional qualifications or accreditations, and the opportunity to build a rewarding career. Trainees are also encouraged to make a difference through volunteering days and community initiatives.

Joining KPMG means working alongside some of the brightest minds in business, and being part of an agile, inclusive environment where everyone is empowered to be their best.

GRADUATE VACANCIES IN 2021
ACCOUNTANCY
CONSULTING
FINANCE
GENERAL MANAGEMENT
HUMAN RESOURCES
LAW
TECHNOLOGY

NUMBER OF VACANCIES
700+ graduate jobs

LOCATIONS OF VACANCIES

STARTING SALARY FOR 2021
£Competitive
Plus a great range of rewards and benefits – see website for details.

UNIVERSITY PROMOTIONS DURING 2020-2021
ABERDEEN, ASTON, BATH, BIRMINGHAM, BRISTOL, CAMBRIDGE, CARDIFF, CITY, DUNDEE, DURHAM, EDINBURGH, ESSEX, EXETER, GLASGOW, HERIOT-WATT, IMPERIAL COLLEGE LONDON, KING'S COLLEGE LONDON, LANCASTER, LEEDS, LEICESTER, LIVERPOOL, LONDON SCHOOL OF ECONOMICS, LOUGHBOROUGH, MANCHESTER, NEWCASTLE, NORTHUMBRIA, NOTTINGHAM, NOTTINGHAM TRENT, OXFORD, PLYMOUTH, QUEEN MARY LONDON, READING, ROYAL HOLLOWAY, SHEFFIELD, SOUTHAMPTON, ST ANDREWS, STRATHCLYDE, SURREY, UEA, UNIVERSITY COLLEGE LONDON, WARWICK, YORK
Please check with your university careers service for full details of KPMG's local promotions and events.

MINIMUM ENTRY REQUIREMENTS
2.1 Degree
Degree in any discipline.

120 UCAS points
300 UCAS points for those who passed exams before 2017.
Please see website for details.

APPLICATION DEADLINE
Year-round recruitment
Early application advised.

FURTHER INFORMATION
www.Top100GraduateEmployers.com
Register now for the latest news, local promotions, work experience and graduate vacancies at KPMG.

Light up your potential

2021 graduate and undergraduate opportunities

Audit, Tax, KPMG Law, Consulting, Deal Advisory, Technology & Engineering

At KPMG, see where your potential takes you. The story of our firm in the UK began 150 years ago, and you could be part of writing our next chapter. Our Audit work helps to build the trust and confidence our economy needs to thrive. In our Advisory business, we work side-by-side with organisations, helping them navigate change and solve some of their most complex challenges.

You'll have the opportunity to make a difference; using your natural curiosity, digital mindset and a desire to work together to explore new ideas and deliver exceptional results. In return, we'll empower you to be your best. Join us and light up a career full of possibilities.

kpmgcareers.co.uk

Together, we achieve more.

KPMG | 150 years supporting the UK

L'ORÉAL

L'Oréal is the world's number one beauty company, with a portfolio of 36 international brands including L'Oréal Paris, Garnier and Lancôme, to name a few. L'Oréal's ambition is to become the world's leading beauty tech company, through digital innovation, product design and world-class consumer journeys.

L'Oréal UK and Ireland, the local subsidiary and leading player in the multi-billion pound beauty industry in the UK, look for an entrepreneurial mind-set in their graduates. They also believe in developing their people from the ground up, providing their employees with the opportunity to grow within the company and build a career with them. As a result, a portion of management trainee roles are filled by individuals from their internship and spring insight programmes, creating a well-rounded junior talent journey at L'Oréal. The remainder of the graduate roles are sourced from the external market, to ensure an equal opportunity for all potential candidates to join this exciting business.

On the Management Trainee Programme, graduates work in functions across the business, gaining a sense of life at L'Oréal. With three different rotations in their chosen stream, graduates are free to develop their talent and discover new possibilities, shaping their future careers as they go. With on-the-job training and their own HR Sponsor, graduates will progress into operational roles in as little as 18 months.

L'Oréal UKI is committed to being one of the top employers in the UK, fostering a workplace where everyone feels welcome and valued. Promoting gender equality, driving diversity and inclusion, addressing mental health and establishing evolving workplace practices are a key focus. Through 'Sharing Beauty with All', L'Oréal's global sustainability programme, the business is driving change across all areas including product design, packaging, supply chain and consumer behaviour.

GRADUATE VACANCIES IN 2021
GENERAL MANAGEMENT
MARKETING
SALES

NUMBER OF VACANCIES
28 graduate jobs

LOCATIONS OF VACANCIES

STARTING SALARY FOR 2021
£30,000

UNIVERSITY PROMOTIONS DURING 2020-2021
BATH, BIRMINGHAM, CAMBRIDGE, TRINITY COLLEGE DUBLIN, UNIVERSITY COLLEGE DUBLIN, DURHAM, EDINBURGH, EXETER, LANCASTER, LEEDS, LIVERPOOL, LONDON SCHOOL OF ECONOMICS, LOUGHBOROUGH, MANCHESTER, NEWCASTLE, OXFORD, OXFORD BROOKES, READING, SUSSEX, UNIVERSITY COLLEGE LONDON, WARWICK, YORK
Please check with your university careers service for full details of L'Oréal's local promotions and events.

APPLICATION DEADLINE
Year-round recruitment
Early application advised.

FURTHER INFORMATION
www.Top100GraduateEmployers.com
Register now for the latest news, local promotions, work experience and graduate vacancies at L'Oréal.

YOU DON'T NEED A SMOKEY EYE
TO BLAZE A TRAIL

But you do need to create engaging social content with our Influencers, predict social trends, and spot the latest trends whilst travelling the world.

At L'Oreal we believe that the diversity of our talent creates the best in beauty.
YOU DON'T NEED TO WEAR MAKE-UP TO MAKE IT

L'ORÉAL   CAREERS.LOREAL.COM

Lidl are proud pioneers in the world of retail. With over 800 stores, 13 warehouses and 25,000 employees in the UK alone, they're one of the fastest growing retailers in the country and are committed to feeding the nation. With their ambitious expansion growth plans, it's clear they don't like to stand still.

Continually challenging and changing the world of grocery retail, Lidl are striving to make the experience exceptional for all, from its customers to its colleagues. Lidl is committed to driving various responsibility programmes, including charity partnerships, food redistribution, recycling schemes and sustainability sourcing for the future.

Lidl is a performance-driven business, and that's exactly what they are looking for in their graduates. They are not looking for one type of person. They are looking for ambitious, committed people with personality and potential. Potential to become one of Lidl's future leaders.

Lidl's structured graduate programmes across all areas of the business are designed to develop graduates quickly by challenging them to reach their potential. They have exciting opportunities for ambitious people who want to join their busy environment, where they'll be challenged to make progress and provide what people need.

Throughout each individual role, graduates will gain soft skills and operational development through a carefully structured training plan, giving a clear development path. Graduates will learn from the best managers and develop their operational and management abilities from day one - progression from there is down to the individual.

Graduates benefit from competitive salaries, fast-tracked development and stimulating work with world-class teams.

GRADUATE VACANCIES IN 2021

GENERAL MANAGEMENT

LOGISTICS

PURCHASING

RETAILING

SALES

NUMBER OF VACANCIES
60 graduate jobs

LOCATIONS OF VACANCIES

STARTING SALARY FOR 2021
£37,000
Plus a company car for selected programmes.

UNIVERSITY PROMOTIONS DURING 2020-2021
Please check with your university careers service for full details of Lidl's local promotions and events.

MINIMUM ENTRY REQUIREMENTS
2.2 Degree

APPLICATION DEADLINE
Varies by function

FURTHER INFORMATION
www.Top100GraduateEmployers.com
Register now for the latest news, local promotions, work experience and graduate vacancies at Lidl.

Choose your future.

Our graduate programmes give huge variety, all-round experience and the skills to grow a career that's going places.

Bring your best. We'll do the rest.

Apply for a career a Lidl less ordinary.

 lidlgraduatecareers.co.uk

Linklaters

From a shifting geopolitical landscape to the exponential growth in FinTech, this is a time of unprecedented change. Linklaters is ready. They go further to support clients, with market-leading legal insight and innovation. And they go further for each other, too.

When people join Linklaters, they find colleagues they want to work with. Inspiring, personable professionals who are generous with their time and always happy to help. Because, to be best in class, Linklaters looks for open minded, team-spirited individuals who will collaborate – and innovate – to deliver the smartest solutions for clients. Linklaters recruits candidates from a range of different backgrounds and disciplines, not just law. Why? Because those candidates bring with them a set of unique skills and perspectives that can help to challenge conventional thinking and inspire different approaches to client problems.

All Linklaters trainees benefit from pioneering learning and development opportunities, and an inclusive working culture that encourages them to fulfil their potential.

Over two years, trainees take four six-month seats (placements) in different practice areas and sometimes abroad. They work on high-profile deals across a global network of 30 offices, and gain the knowledge they need to qualify. And throughout their career, they enjoy the advantage of world-class training, courtesy of the Linklaters Learning & Development team.

With their uniquely future-focused culture and high-profile, global opportunities, Linklaters provides the ideal preparation for a rewarding career, no matter what the future holds.

Great change is here. Get ready.

GRADUATE VACANCIES IN 2021
LAW

NUMBER OF VACANCIES
100 graduate jobs
For training contracts starting in 2023.

LOCATIONS OF VACANCIES

STARTING SALARY FOR 2021
£47,000

UNIVERSITY PROMOTIONS DURING 2020-2021
BELFAST, BIRMINGHAM, BRISTOL, CAMBRIDGE, CITY, TRINITY COLLEGE DUBLIN, UNIVERSITY COLLEGE DUBLIN, DURHAM, EDINBURGH, EXETER, GLASGOW, KING'S COLLEGE LONDON, KENT, LANCASTER, LEEDS, LEICESTER, LONDON SCHOOL OF ECONOMICS, MANCHESTER, NOTTINGHAM, NOTTINGHAM TRENT, OXFORD, OXFORD BROOKES, QUEEN MARY LONDON, SCHOOL OF AFRICAN STUDIES, SHEFFIELD, ST ANDREWS, SURREY, SUSSEX, UEA, UNIVERSITY COLLEGE LONDON, WARWICK, YORK
Please check with your university careers service for full details of Linklaters' local promotions and events.

MINIMUM ENTRY REQUIREMENTS
2.1 Degree

APPLICATION DEADLINE
10th December 2020

FURTHER INFORMATION
www.Top100GraduateEmployers.com
*Register now for the latest news, local promotions, work experience and graduate vacancies at **Linklaters**.*

Great change is here.

Linklaters

Are you ready?

From a shifting geopolitical landscape
to the exponential growth in FinTech,
this is a time of unprecedented change.

At Linklaters, we're ready. Our people
go further to support our clients,
with market-leading legal insight and
innovation. And we go further for each
other, too. We're people you want to work
with, generous with our time and ready
to help. So no matter what the future
holds, with us you'll be one step ahead.
Great change is here. Get ready.

Find out more at careers.linklaters.com

As the UK's largest retail and digital bank, with over 26 million customers, Lloyds Banking Group offers graduates a wide range of opportunities to make a real impact for customers, communities and colleagues through brands like Lloyds Bank, Halifax, Scottish Widows and Bank of Scotland.

The banking world is changing fast. New technology and new opportunities are affecting how people bank every day. To become the bank of the future and meet the ever-changing needs of their customers, Lloyds Banking Group is inviting graduates with a wide range of skills and experience to embark on a career with them.

Lloyds Banking Group is looking for graduates who are excited by rewarding challenges, who thrive in an inclusive culture and are inspired by the Group's purpose of helping Britain prosper. Whether it's forming relationships with clients or developing the next generation of technology, graduates will be given opportunities to make a real difference for customers, communities and colleagues.

At Lloyds Banking Group there are a variety of graduate schemes and internships. Whether they choose Commercial Banking, Data Science or Risk Management, graduates will be supported to achieve a relevant professional qualification or training, all with the support of buddies and their teams.

Best of all, Lloyds Banking Group offers a friendly and supportive work environment, where balance is valued, flexible working patterns and ongoing well-being support are championed, and everyone feels free to be themselves.

This is because Lloyds Banking Group knows that people do their best work when they feel respected and happy.

Discover careers with real impact at Lloyds Banking Group.

GRADUATE VACANCIES IN 2021

ACCOUNTANCY
ENGINEERING
FINANCE
MARKETING
TECHNOLOGY

NUMBER OF VACANCIES
100+ graduate jobs

LOCATIONS OF VACANCIES

STARTING SALARY FOR 2021
£31,000-£45,000
Plus a discretionary bonus, a settling-in allowance and flexible working.

UNIVERSITY PROMOTIONS DURING 2020-2021
ASTON, BIRMINGHAM, BRISTOL, CAMBRIDGE, CARDIFF, DUNDEE, EDINBURGH, EXETER, GLASGOW, IMPERIAL COLLEGE LONDON, KING'S COLLEGE LONDON, LEEDS, LIVERPOOL, LONDON SCHOOL OF ECONOMICS, MANCHESTER, NEWCASTLE, NOTTINGHAM, OXFORD, QUEEN MARY LONDON, STRATHCLYDE, UNIVERSITY COLLEGE LONDON, WARWICK, YORK
Please check with your university careers service for full details of Lloyds Banking Group's local promotions and events.

MINIMUM ENTRY REQUIREMENTS
2.2 Degree

APPLICATION DEADLINE
Varies by function

FURTHER INFORMATION
www.Top100GraduateEmployers.com
Register now for the latest news, local promotions, work experience and vacancies at Lloyds Banking Group.

Physics degree

Data Science Programme

"I'm building safe AI products for millions"

400 hours Python coding training

WHAT IMPACT WILL YOU MAKE?

We look beyond areas of study because we know that diverse skillsets are essential to great work. Daniel's LBG journey started with an internship and he now develops technology that transforms people's lives. Start your journey here – and join us in helping Britain prosper.

Discover careers with real impact at
lloydsbankinggrouptalent.com

M&S is changing for good. They've always been a retail innovator, creating industry-first customer experiences. Now, with changing customer habits, M&S are revolutionising retail by combining their creativity and digital know-how with their exceptional commitment to sustainability.

Whether it's their exciting product development, sustainable packaging or ethical supply chains, M&S is leading by example when it comes to good business. They're looking for graduates who want nothing more than to make a big, positive impact on communities. Graduates who appreciate the growing importance retail has in society and its ability to change the world for the better.

Undertaking this challenge will be a thrill to those with real ambition. Graduates will have the opportunity to link up with influential members of the business and hash out smarter ways of doing things. From delighting customers to reinventing product ranges and improving financial performance.

M&S offers a range of specialised programmes including Store Management, Clothing Design, Food Technology, and Buying and Merchandising. Each offers unique opportunities to learn on business-critical projects, build expertise and network with inspiring colleagues.

There's also an Enterprise programme available to the most strategically minded, entrepreneurially spirited business minds. It's perfect for those who are proactive and show real leadership potential.

Whichever path they take, graduates will enjoy a competitive salary, great benefits and real opportunities to grow. They'll also be encouraged to demonstrate their ability to put customers at the heart of everything, push the boundaries and think about the bigger picture of the business.

GRADUATE VACANCIES IN 2021

CONSULTING

GENERAL MANAGEMENT

MARKETING

PURCHASING

RETAILING

NUMBER OF VACANCIES
30 graduate jobs

LOCATIONS OF VACANCIES

STARTING SALARY FOR 2021
£Competitive

UNIVERSITY PROMOTIONS DURING 2020-2021
BATH, BELFAST, BIRMINGHAM, GLASGOW, LANCASTER, LEEDS, LOUGHBOROUGH, MANCHESTER, NEWCASTLE, NOTTINGHAM TRENT, OXFORD BROOKES, READING
Please check with your university careers service for full details of M&S's local promotions and events.

APPLICATION DEADLINE
Late November 2020

FURTHER INFORMATION
www.Top100GraduateEmployers.com
Register now for the latest news, local promotions, work experience and graduate vacancies at M&S.

MARS

GRADUATE VACANCIES IN 2021

ENGINEERING
FINANCE
GENERAL MANAGEMENT
HUMAN RESOURCES
MARKETING
PURCHASING
RESEARCH & DEVELOPMENT
SALES

NUMBER OF VACANCIES
25 graduate jobs

LOCATIONS OF VACANCIES

Vacancies also available in Europe and elsewhere in the world.

STARTING SALARY FOR 2021
£32,000
Plus a £2,000 joining bonus.

UNIVERSITY PROMOTIONS DURING 2020-2021
BATH, BIRMINGHAM, CAMBRIDGE, DURHAM, EXETER, LEEDS, NOTTINGHAM, OXFORD, WARWICK
Please check with your university careers service for full details of Mars' local promotions and events.

MINIMUM ENTRY REQUIREMENTS
2.1 Degree

APPLICATION DEADLINE
Varies by function

FURTHER INFORMATION
www.Top100GraduateEmployers.com
Register now for the latest news, local promotions, work experience and graduate vacancies at Mars.

Think Maltesers®, M&Ms®, Uncle Ben's®, Pedigree®, Whiskas® and Extra®, some of the nation's best-loved and well-known brands. Think the world's third-largest food company, with 115,000 associates and international operations across the world. Know what makes Mars special? Think again.

Sure, Mars is one of the world's leading food companies, but it's more like a community than a corporate – because it's still a private, family-owned business built up of a Mars family of associates. Associates at Mars are united and guided by The Five Principles – Quality, Responsibility, Mutuality, Efficiency and Freedom. These are key to the culture and help associates to make business decisions they are proud of.

The culture at Mars is relationship-driven – and it's how these relationships are built that's most important. Collaborating with others is key to getting things done. Mars encourages open communication as this builds relationships of trust and respect.

Mars want to stretch and challenge associates every day to help them reach their full potential. So they take learning and development seriously – it makes good business sense for Mars to have people performing at the top of their game. With great managers, mentors, coaches and peers, graduates will be supported the whole way. And they will support other associates on their journey too.

At Mars, graduates are offered an unrivalled opportunity to make a difference in their roles from day one. Mars wants everything they do to matter – from the smallest thing to the biggest – and Mars wants their work to make a positive difference to customers, suppliers, associates and the world as a whole. Graduates will have endless support to develop both personally and professionally, creating a start to an exciting and fulfilling career.

Make reading this the start of your career.

Ready for a Mars Leadership Experience?

The future you want tomorrow starts with the decision you make today. Each of our 10,000 Associates were once where you are now, deciding if Mars is the right place to build a future. If you're ready to manage projects, build trust, take on real roles with local and international exposure, then one of our Mars Leadership Experiences could be exactly what you've been looking for. So, get ready to collaborate, seize a great development opportunity and make a difference – today and every day.

Make today count, visit
Mars.co.uk/graduates

#TomorrowStartsToday

SECURITYSERVICE
MI5

mi5.gov.uk/careers

GRADUATE VACANCIES IN 2021
GENERAL MANAGEMENT
INTELLIGENCE GATHERING
TECHNOLOGY

NUMBER OF VACANCIES
200+ graduate jobs

LOCATIONS OF VACANCIES

STARTING SALARY FOR 2021
£32,655+

**UNIVERSITY PROMOTIONS
DURING 2020-2021**
*Please check with your university careers
service for full details of MI5's local
promotions and events.*

MINIMUM ENTRY REQUIREMENTS
2.2 Degree

APPLICATION DEADLINE
Varies by function

FURTHER INFORMATION
www.Top100GraduateEmployers.com
*Register now for the latest news, local
promotions, work experience and
graduate vacancies at MI5.*

MI5 helps safeguard the UK against threats to national security including terrorism and espionage. It investigates suspect individuals and organisations to gather intelligence relating to security threats. MI5 also advises the critical national infrastructure on protective security measures.

Graduates from a range of backgrounds join MI5 for stimulating and rewarding careers, in a supportive environment, whilst enjoying a good work-life balance. Many graduates join the Intelligence Officer Development Programme, which is a structured four year programme designed to teach new joiners about MI5 investigations and give them the skills to run them. After completing one post of two years, or two posts of one year, in areas which teach aspects of intelligence work, and subject to successful completion of a final assessment, graduates will then take up an investigative post as a fully trained Intelligence Officer.

MI5 also deals with vast amounts of data, and interpreting that data is vital to its intelligence work. The Intelligence and Data Analyst Development Programme is a structured five-year programme which prepares individuals with potential to be part of this specialist career stream. It will take them from the basics through to the most innovative data analytical techniques. As they progress, they will use their analytical expertise in different teams across a range of MI5 investigations.

MI5 also offers a structured Technology Graduate Development Programme, which gives graduates the experience, knowledge and skills they need to be an effective technology professional in the organisation's pioneering IT function.

Graduates who are looking for a rewarding career in corporate services can join MI5 as Business Enablers, where they can develop a breadth of experience undertaking corporate roles across a range of business areas, before having the opportunity to specialise in a particular area.

YOUR
POTENTIAL IS
GREATER THAN
FICTION

Intelligence Officer
Development Programme

**£32,655, rising to £35,301
after one year**

You might think that working for MI5 as an Intelligence Officer is the stuff of imagination. But it's a real job for real people. In fact, we need individuals from a diverse range of backgrounds to bring different perspectives and experiences to the role.

You might assume that you don't have what it takes but you could well have the attributes we're looking for. We need people with excellent communication skills, who enjoy problem solving and have the ability to see the bigger picture. We'll teach you the rest through a structured development programme where you'll learn how to help keep the country safe. And while you might think it's a stressful, intense job, it's actually all about team-work and the environment is incredibly supportive. You also can't take your work home with you, so that's the work-life balance sorted!

MI5 is committed to equal opportunities and to reflecting the society we protect. All applications are welcome, but we particularly welcome applications from women and Black, Asian and Minority Ethnic candidates.

To enjoy one of the most rewarding careers you can imagine, find out more about the Intelligence Officer Development Programme at **www.mi5.gov.uk/careers**

SECURITYSERVICE
MI5

Morgan Stanley

morganstanley.com/campus

facebook.com/MorganStanley [f] graduaterecruitmenteurope@morganstanley.com [✉]

linkedin.com/company/morgan-stanley [in] twitter.com/MorganStanley [y]

instagram.com/Morgan.Stanley [○] youtube.com/MorganStanley [▶]

Morgan Stanley is one of the world's leading financial services firms. They generate, manage and distribute capital, helping businesses get the funds they need to develop innovative products and services that benefit millions. Their work is defined by the passion and dedication of their people, and their goals are achieved through hiring, training and rewarding the best possible talent.

At Morgan Stanley attitude is just as important as aptitude, and they want to work with and develop students and graduates who show integrity and commitment to their core values, who share their commitment to providing first-class client service, and who embrace change and innovation. Because the firm values a diversity of perspectives, it encourages people to be themselves and pursue their own interests.

There are numerous opportunities to learn, grow professionally and help put the power of capital to work. All of Morgan Stanley's programmes are designed to provide the knowledge and toolkit graduates need to develop quickly into an effective and successful professional in their chosen area. Training is not limited to the first weeks or months on the job, but continues throughout a graduate's career. Over time, they could become part of the next generation of leaders, and play a part in technological, scientific and cultural advancements that change the world forever.

Morgan Stanley believes that capital can work to benefit all. This success needs financial capital, but its foundation is intellectual capital. The talents and points of view of the diverse individuals working for them help to build their legacy and shape their future. This is why Morgan Stanley accepts applicants from all degree disciplines who demonstrate academic excellence.

GRADUATE VACANCIES IN 2021

FINANCE

HUMAN RESOURCES

INVESTMENT BANKING

TECHNOLOGY

NUMBER OF VACANCIES
200+ graduate jobs

LOCATIONS OF VACANCIES

STARTING SALARY FOR 2021
£Competitive

**UNIVERSITY PROMOTIONS
DURING 2020-2021**
Please check with your university careers service for full details of Morgan Stanley's local promotions and events.

MINIMUM ENTRY REQUIREMENTS
*Strong academic background,
2.1 or equivalent preferred.*

APPLICATION DEADLINE
Varies by function

FURTHER INFORMATION
www.Top100GraduateEmployers.com
*Register now for the latest news, local
promotions, work experience and
graduate vacancies at **Morgan Stanley**.*

WE ARE
Morgan Stanley

We are defined by our people, our founders, our company veterans and our newest recruits.

We draw on the strength of their diverse talents and perspectives, generating growth for our clients in ways that are forward-thinking and sustainable.

We collaborate across departments and our global network of offices to deliver exceptional ideas and solutions to the world's most complex challenges.

morganstanley.com/campus

MOTT MACDONALD

mottmac.com/careers/uk-and-ireland-graduate
facebook.com/MottMacdonaldGroup **f**   earlycareers.recruitment@mottmac.com ✉
linkedin.com/company/mott-macdonald **in**   twitter.com/MottMacLife 🐦
instagram.com/MottMacGroup 📷   youtube.com/MottMacdonald ▶

Mott MacDonald is a global engineering, management and development consultancy focused on guiding clients through many of the planet's most intricate challenges. By challenging norms and unlocking creativity, Mott MacDonald delivers long-lasting value for societies around the globe.

Improvement is at the heart of what Mott MacDonald offers. Better economic development, better social and environmental outcomes, better businesses and a better return on investment. Their 16,000-strong network of experts are joined-up across sectors and geographies, giving their graduates access to an exceptional breadth and depth of expertise and experience, enhancing their knowledge with the right support and guidance every step of the way. The consultancy's employees, active in 150 countries, take leading roles on some of the world's highest profile projects, turning obstacles into elegant, sustainable solutions. Individuals who get satisfaction from working on projects that benefit communities around the world will thrive at Mott MacDonald. Additionally, as Mott MacDonald is an employee-owned company, it allows them to choose the work they take on and focus on the issues that are important.

Mott MacDonald's graduate schemes are more than just graduate jobs. With the help of a dedicated learning and development team, the accredited schemes aim to give graduates the opportunity to continually progress and develop in their chosen field. With learning and development being a constant focus throughout a graduate's career at Mott MacDonald, the schemes have been created specifically to enable graduates to be the best that they can be. All entry-level professionals are enrolled in Accelerating Your Future, a structured development programme that introduces key business and commercial competencies.

GRADUATE VACANCIES IN 2021
CONSULTING
ENGINEERING
TECHNOLOGY

NUMBER OF VACANCIES
200 graduate jobs

LOCATIONS OF VACANCIES

STARTING SALARY FOR 2021
£28,000

UNIVERSITY PROMOTIONS DURING 2020-2021
Please check with your university careers service for full details of Mott MacDonald's local promotions and events.

APPLICATION DEADLINE
20th November 2020

FURTHER INFORMATION
www.Top100GraduateEmployers.com
Register now for the latest news, local promotions, work experience and graduate vacancies at Mott MacDonald.

Changing their name from RBS to NatWest Group was an important step on their journey to create a truly purpose-led bank. They believe they succeed when their customers and their communities succeed as well. This is their purpose: to champion potential; helping people, families and businesses to thrive.

Graduate and Intern programmes at NatWest Group offer structured and supported learning, making sure student potential comes first. With pathways allowing candidates to join the part of the business that suits them best, people can build a career they'll love. Their people are the foundation that their success is built on, so they help colleagues to thrive by promising a fulfilling role, fair pay, excellent training and great leadership.

Focusing on things they believe everyone shares – the need for financial security, the desire to improve a person's place in society, and the environment everyone lives in – NatWest Group aims to empower individuals and communities wherever they are. They use their expertise to share knowledge and skills which help people improve their financial wellbeing, through initiatives such as their long-standing MoneySense programme. They open doors to business and encourage entrepreneurship, particularly among underrepresented groups. And they're a major funder of renewable energy projects, while driving their own operations to carbon positive.

Colleagues will benefit from an inclusive culture where individual strengths and working styles are appreciated and encouraged. And because of their significant investment in technology, no matter where people or their colleagues are based, working at NatWest Group is more flexible than it's ever been. Graduates and Interns collaborate across the organisation; getting the support they need to make a positive impact with the work they do.

GRADUATE VACANCIES IN 2021

FINANCE

HUMAN RESOURCES

MARKETING

TECHNOLOGY

NUMBER OF VACANCIES

228 graduate jobs

LOCATIONS OF VACANCIES

STARTING SALARY FOR 2021

£31,850

Plus benefits.

UNIVERSITY PROMOTIONS DURING 2020-2021

ASTON, BIRMINGHAM, BRISTOL, DURHAM, EDINBURGH, GLASGOW, HERIOT-WATT, LEEDS, MANCHESTER, NOTTINGHAM, QUEEN MARY LONDON, SHEFFIELD, ST ANDREWS, STRATHCLYDE, UNIVERSITY COLLEGE LONDON, WARWICK

Please check with your university careers service for full details of NatWest Group's local promotions and events.

MINIMUM ENTRY REQUIREMENTS

2.1 Degree

APPLICATION DEADLINE

31st December 2020

FURTHER INFORMATION

www.Top100GraduateEmployers.com

*Register now for the latest news, local promotions, work experience and graduate vacancies at **NatWest Group**.*

We champion potential.

NatWest Group

Our purpose is to help people, families and businesses to thrive.

We want to build deep, lasting relationships with our customers – that's the best way for us to help them succeed. When our customers succeed, we succeed and become what people want us to be – resilient, sustainable and built for the long-term.

We know we're on a journey, but we're determined to see it through.

To help us achieve our purpose, we promise you a clear and fulfilling job – where you can be yourself, achieve a healthy work-life balance and see your career flourish.

Visit jobs.natwestgroup.com to explore our graduate and intern programmes.

Network Rail own and operate the railway infrastructure in England, Scotland and Wales. Their purpose is to create a better railway for a better Britain. It is the fastest growing and safest rail network in Europe, presenting an abundance of opportunities for ambitious and enthusiastic graduates.

Network Rail have £47bn earmarked to invest in landmark projects and initiatives as part of their Railway Upgrade Plan. They are already making history through some of the largest engineering projects in Europe: Crossrail, Birmingham New Street Station, London Bridge, HS2 and Thameslink.

Although rail is a huge part of their business, they are also one of the largest land and property owners in Britain. They manage a portfolio that includes 18 of the biggest stations in Britain, the retail outlets inside them and the small businesses that live under their arches.

Network Rail are looking to invest in graduates who are committed to making a difference, to help transform Britain's rail infrastructure, transport network and economy for the 22nd century.

They have supported thousands of graduates through their diverse and challenging programmes. Graduates will have access to Westwood, their state-of-the-art training centre in Coventry, and six other training facilities.

There are two entry routes for graduates. Within Engineering there are three specific schemes: civil, electrical & electronic, and mechanical engineering.

In Business Management, applicants can choose from the following schemes: finance, general management, health, safety and environment, HR, IT & business services, project management, property and quantity surveying.

There are also summer and year in industry placements available for those who would like to find out what it is like to work for Network Rail before graduation.

GRADUATE VACANCIES IN 2021
ENGINEERING
FINANCE
GENERAL MANAGEMENT
HUMAN RESOURCES
PROPERTY
PURCHASING

NUMBER OF VACANCIES
150+ graduate jobs

LOCATIONS OF VACANCIES

STARTING SALARY FOR 2021
£26,500
Plus a £2,000 welcome bonus.

UNIVERSITY PROMOTIONS DURING 2020-2021
ASTON, BATH, BIRMINGHAM, LEEDS, LEICESTER, LIVERPOOL, LOUGHBOROUGH, MANCHESTER, NOTTINGHAM, NOTTINGHAM TRENT, SHEFFIELD, STRATHCLYDE, YORK
Please check with your university careers service for full details of Network Rail's local promotions and events.

MINIMUM ENTRY REQUIREMENTS
2.2 Degree

FURTHER INFORMATION
www.Top100GraduateEmployers.com
Register now for the latest news, local promotions, work experience and graduate vacancies at Network Rail.

NEWTON

Newton isn't like most consultancies. At Newton, consultants are called in to crack some of the toughest challenges that businesses and public sector organisations face. They hire people with spirit, personality and bravery - and go to extraordinary lengths to build their skills and belief.

Newton trust the ingenuity of their people so deeply that they put their fee at risk to guarantee results for clients. And they believe in the impact of the solutions they create so much that they promise to stay on in each clients' businesses to make sure they get the results they need.

The business model is bold and disruptive – and it doesn't make things easy for consultants on the ground. But it does make things interesting. They regularly encounter problems and complexities that haven't been tackled before, and they don't have pre-fabricated answers to fall back on. They have to rely not just on their combined knowledge, but on their own courage, passion and self-belief.

They've already achieved amazing things as a team. For one retail client, they grew top line sales by £¼ bn and took 80,000 people through a change programme. On a major UK defence build programme, they saw a 64% improvement in cost performance. And elsewhere they've reduced Child in Need and Child Protection caseload numbers by 29%.

Newton are looking for extraordinary people to join as Operations Consultants and Digital Consultants. All consultants work alongside a variety of clients to design and implement programmes that deliver sustainable change working from the shop floor to the boardroom. They're encouraged to "get stuck right in" and use their initiative and creativity to deliver far-reaching and measurable results for clients, demanding better for them. Newton is an employer where, if graduates don't limit themselves, nothing will limit them.

GRADUATE VACANCIES IN 2021
CONSULTING

NUMBER OF VACANCIES
110 graduate jobs

LOCATIONS OF VACANCIES

STARTING SALARY FOR 2021
£45,000-£50,000 package
Including a £5,000 car allowance.
Plus a sign-on bonus.

UNIVERSITY PROMOTIONS DURING 2020-2021
BATH, BIRMINGHAM, BRISTOL, CAMBRIDGE, DURHAM, EDINBURGH, EXETER, IMPERIAL COLLEGE LONDON, LONDON SCHOOL OF ECONOMICS, MANCHESTER, NOTTINGHAM, OXFORD, ST ANDREWS, STRATHCLYDE, UNIVERSITY COLLEGE LONDON, WARWICK
Please check with your university careers service for full details of Newton's local promotions and events.

APPLICATION DEADLINE
25th December 2020

FURTHER INFORMATION
www.Top100GraduateEmployers.com
Register now for the latest news, local promotions, work experience and graduate vacancies at Newton.

NEVER NOT EMPOWERED.
NEVER NOT NEWTON.

At Newton, we believe that growing starts with doing. So we'll ensure you have a real voice on major projects from the moment you join. Which means you'll have the ability to influence big decisions, create real impact – and significantly grow your potential.

Find out more at **WorkAtNewton.com**

NATIONAL GRADUATE
DEVELOPMENT PROGRAMME

ngdp

FOR LOCAL GOVERNMENT

local.gov.uk/ngdp

ngdp.support@local.gov.uk

linkedin.com/company/ngdp-lga **in**   twitter.com/ngdp_LGA **y**

The ngdp is a two-year graduate development programme which gives committed graduates the opportunity and training to fast-track their career in local government. The ngdp is looking to equip the sector's next generation of high-calibre managers to impact the lives of the people in the communities they serve.

Local government is responsible for a wide range of vital services for communities. They are a diverse and large employer, with more than one million people working in local government, providing more than 800 services. More than 1,300 graduates have completed the ngdp since 1999 and gained access to rewarding careers within and beyond the sector, with many currently holding influential managerial and policy roles.

Ngdp graduates are positioned to make a real contribution to shaping and implementing new ideas and initiatives in local government. Graduate trainees are employed by a participating council (or group of councils) for two years, during which time they rotate between a minimum of three different placements in key areas of the council. Past trainees have developed a cultural education strategy in consultation with residents, worked in partnership with charities to reduce homelessness and project-managed the introduction of new digital initiatives. The exposure to such a wide range of services means participants can gain a flexible, transferable skill set to take beyond the programme.

Ngdp graduates also benefit from being part of a national cohort of peers. Together they participate in a learning and development programme alongside the day job, leading to a post-graduate qualification in Leadership and Management. The programme gives graduates the chance to learn from established professionals and develop their own networks. Join now to start working for change and have a tangible impact from day one.

GRADUATE VACANCIES IN 2021

ACCOUNTANCY
FINANCE
GENERAL MANAGEMENT
HUMAN RESOURCES
LAW
LOGISTICS
MARKETING
MEDIA
PROPERTY
PURCHASING
RESEARCH & DEVELOPMENT
TECHNOLOGY

NUMBER OF VACANCIES
120-150 graduate jobs

LOCATIONS OF VACANCIES

STARTING SALARY FOR 2021
£25,000

**UNIVERSITY PROMOTIONS
DURING 2020-2021**
ASTON, BATH, BIRMINGHAM, BRADFORD, BRISTOL, BRUNEL, CITY, EXETER, KING'S COLLEGE LONDON, KENT, LONDON SCHOOL OF ECONOMICS, MANCHESTER, NORTHUMBRIA, NOTTINGHAM, NOTTINGHAM TRENT, PLYMOUTH, QUEEN MARY LONDON, ROYAL HOLLOWAY, SCHOOL OF AFRICAN STUDIES, SHEFFIELD, SOUTHAMPTON, SURREY, UEA, UNIVERSITY COLLEGE LONDON, WARWICK
Please check with your university careers service for full details of the ngdp's local promotions and events.

MINIMUM ENTRY REQUIREMENTS
2.2 Degree

APPLICATION DEADLINE
January 2021

FURTHER INFORMATION
www.Top100GraduateEmployers.com
Register now for the latest news, local promotions, work experience and graduate vacancies in Local Government.

NHS

Graduate Management Training Scheme

As Europe's largest employer, with an annual budget of over £100 billion, there is no other organisation on earth quite like the NHS. With the ability to have a positive impact on the health and wellbeing of 56 million people, the NHS Graduate Management Training Scheme is a life-defining experience.

Being on this scheme is unquestionably hard work, but this multi-award-winning, fast-track development scheme will enable graduates to become the healthcare leaders of the future. Graduates specialise in one of six areas: finance, general management, human resources, health informatics, policy & strategy and health analysis.

As graduates grow personally and professionally, they'll gain specialist skills while receiving full support from a dedicated mentor at executive level. Every graduate joining the scheme will access a comprehensive learning and development package designed by some of the most experienced and expert learning providers in the UK. Success is granted only to those who are prepared to give their heart and soul to their profession.

The responsibility of the NHS demands that their future leaders have tenacity, focus, and determination to deliver nothing but the best. Because the scheme offers a fast-track route to a senior-level role, graduates will soon find themselves facing complex problems head on and tackling high profile situations.

Working for the NHS means standing up to high levels of public scrutiny and having decisions closely inspected. Graduates who want to succeed will need to be thick-skinned, resilient and able to respond to constant change. This is a career where the hard work and unfaltering commitment of graduates not only affects the lives of others, but will ultimately define their own.

GRADUATE VACANCIES IN 2021

ACCOUNTANCY
FINANCE
GENERAL MANAGEMENT
HUMAN RESOURCES
RESEARCH & DEVELOPMENT
TECHNOLOGY

NUMBER OF VACANCIES
500 graduate jobs

LOCATIONS OF VACANCIES

STARTING SALARY FOR 2021
£24,628

UNIVERSITY PROMOTIONS DURING 2020-2021
Please check with your university careers service for full details of the NHS's local promotions and events.

MINIMUM ENTRY REQUIREMENTS
2.2 Degree

FURTHER INFORMATION
www.Top100GraduateEmployers.com
Register now for the latest news, local promotions, work experience and graduate vacancies at the NHS.

Graduate Management Training Scheme

Supporting frontline care is what we do.

What difference can you make?

The NHS Graduate Management Training Scheme is nothing less than a life-defining experience. Whether you join our finance, general management, health analysis, health informatics, human resources, or policy and strategy scheme, you'll receive everything you need to make a positive impact on the lives of 56 million people across England.

These aren't clinical opportunities, but this is about developing exceptional healthcare leaders. High-calibre management professionals who will lead the NHS through a profound transformation and shape our services around ever-evolving patient needs. Inspirational people who will push up standards, deliver deeper value for money and continue the drive towards a healthier nation.

Visit:
www.nhsgraduates.co.uk

penguinrandomhousecareers.co.uk

facebook.com/PRHcareersUK **f**   PRHcareersUK@penguinrandomhouse.co.uk

@PRHcareersUK   twitter.com/PRHcareersUK **y**

Penguin Random House UK connects the world with the stories, ideas and writing that matter. As the biggest publisher in the UK, the diversity of its publishing includes brands such as Jamie Oliver, James Patterson and Peppa Pig through to literary prize winners such as Zadie Smith and Richard Flanagan.

Career opportunities range from the creative teams in Editorial, Marketing, Publicity and Design through to teams in Digital, Finance, Technology, Sales and Publishing Operations, to name but a few.

The Scheme is Penguin Random House's flagship entry level programme which offers 6-month editorial traineeships to applicants from BAME or low socio-economic backgrounds.

They also run 8-week Summer Internships that are open to all and offer the chance to work in teams from all departments: editorial, marketing, sales and technology. For any vacancies or entry level programmes, there is no degree or educational requirement.

Penguin Random House has nine publishing houses, each distinct, with their own imprints, markets and identity, including a fast-growing Audio publishing division.

They work with a wide range of talent – from storytellers, animators and developers to entrepreneurs, toy manufacturers, producers and, of course, writers. Just like broadcasters, they find increasingly different ways to bring stories and ideas to life.

Penguin Random House UK has two publishing sites in London – Vauxhall Bridge Road and Embassy Gardens; distribution centres in Frating, Grantham and Rugby; and a number of regional offices. They employ over 2,000 people in the UK.

GRADUATE VACANCIES IN 2021

MARKETING
MEDIA
SALES

NUMBER OF VACANCIES
200+ entry-level roles

LOCATIONS OF VACANCIES

STARTING SALARY FOR 2021
£24,000

UNIVERSITY PROMOTIONS DURING 2020-2021
Please check with your university careers service for full details of Penguin Random House's local promotions and events.

APPLICATION DEADLINE
Year-round recruitment

FURTHER INFORMATION
www.Top100GraduateEmployers.com
Register now for the latest news, local promotions, work experience and graduate vacancies at Penguin.

Your Story Starts Here

Finding a great story - editor, publisher, sales director, finance team. Making it look good - designer, copy writer, art director, illustrator. Making the finished book - production controller, product manager, quality controller. Getting it out there - marketing assistant, publicity manager, sales executive, social media manager.

Come and be part of the first of a new kind of publisher that captures the attention of the world through the stories, ideas and writing that matter.

Penguin
Random House
UK

graduate.pinsentmasons.com
facebook.com/PMgrads **f**   graduate@pinsentmasons.com ✉
instagram.com/PM_grads ⃝   twitter.com/PMgrads **y**

GRADUATE VACANCIES IN 2021
LAW

NUMBER OF VACANCIES
60-70 graduate jobs
For training contracts starting in 2023.

LOCATIONS OF VACANCIES

Pinsent Masons is an international law firm with a reputation for delivering high-quality legal advice, rooted in its deep understanding of the sectors and geographies in which our clients operate. The firm employs over 3,500 people worldwide, including around 1,800 lawyers and 480 partners.

Pinsent Masons is a global 100 law firm, with a sector-led approach specialising in the energy, infrastructure, financial services, real estate and technology, science and industry.

The firm's international footprint encompasses seven offices across Asia Pacific, two offices in the Middle East, fifteen offices in continental Europe and one in Africa. Pinsent Masons also has comprehensive coverage across each of the UK's three legal jurisdictions.

Penultimate year law students, or final year non-law students, can apply for the Vacation Placement. Over the course of a number of weeks, attendees will be fully immersed in all aspects of working life at Pinsent Masons. Placement students will experience a structured programme of work-based learning, skills training and presentations, as well as plenty of socialising and networking. The programme is available across all of our UK offices.

Pinsent Masons' two-year Training Contract comprises four six-month seats, spent in different Practice Groups, and combines regulatory and skills training. Seat allocations take account of trainees' preferences and aim to strike a balance between their choices and the firm's requirements. In each seat, trainees will be supervised by a senior colleague who will guide them through their learning and development. There is also full support from Pinsent Masons' Graduate Development team, who will meet trainees regularly to discuss their on-going performance.

STARTING SALARY FOR 2021
£24,000-£41,000
Plus a comprehensive benefits package.

UNIVERSITY PROMOTIONS DURING 2020-2021
Please check with your university careers service for full details of Pinsent Masons' local promotions and events.

MINIMUM ENTRY REQUIREMENTS
2.1 Degree
120 UCAS points
300+ UCAS points for those who passed exams before 2017.

APPLICATION DEADLINE
Varies by function

FURTHER INFORMATION
www.Top100GraduateEmployers.com
*Register now for the latest news, local promotions, work experience and graduate vacancies at **Pinsent Masons**.*

TAKE THE LAW INTO YOUR OWN HANDS

We're not just one of The Times Top 100 Graduate Employers. Last year we were The Legal Business Awards' Law Firm of the Year and our people around the world continue to work together to realise our even bigger ambitions. So there's nowhere better to take your legal career into your own hands.

Our training contracts are unlike any other: giving you experience-building responsibility and client exposure, supported by personalised career coaching that's unique to Pinsent Masons.

It all begins with a comprehensive induction to get you off to the confident start essential to making the most of the career paths open to you across the UK and around the world.

Ready to start as you mean to go on?

pinsentmasons.com/graduates

#takethelaw

GRADUATE VACANCIES IN 2021
POLICING

NUMBER OF VACANCIES
660+ graduate jobs

LOCATIONS OF VACANCIES

STARTING SALARY FOR 2021
£23,124
Average starting salary for 2020 cohort.

UNIVERSITY PROMOTIONS DURING 2020-2021
Please check with your university careers service for full details of Police Now's local promotions and events.

MINIMUM ENTRY REQUIREMENTS
2.2 Degree
Plus a C grade in English at GCSE.

APPLICATION DEADLINE
Year-round recruitment
Early application advised.

FURTHER INFORMATION
www.Top100GraduateEmployers.com
Register now for the latest news, local promotions, work experience and graduate vacancies at Police Now.

Police Now is a charity with a mission to transform communities by recruiting, developing and inspiring leaders in policing. Diversity and inclusion matters; therefore, they aim to recruit high-achieving graduates from diverse backgrounds, especially those who might not have previously considered policing.

Since 2015, Police Now has recruited, trained and developed over 1,000 police officers, posting them in neighbourhood roles in some of England and Wales' most deprived communities. Their outstanding participants play an important role in supporting the nation's police in their efforts to increase the number of officers across England and Wales, and to drive positive change. It is important to have police officers as diverse as the communities that they serve, across the nation, and they have made it their mission to push this agenda.

Police Now's National Graduate Leadership Programme offers a career opportunity like no other. As a neighbourhood police officer, graduates will develop leadership skills for life. They will be placed in a unique and challenging environment, where they will make a real and lasting difference to some of the most vulnerable communities in England and Wales.

Throughout the two-year programme, they will be visible leaders in their community. They will develop skills in negotiation, problem-solving, decision-making, and emotional intelligence in their role as neighbourhood police officers.

At the end of the two years, they will have a number of exciting opportunities waiting for them. They'll be able to continue in a neighbourhood policing role, move to one of the other vast arrays of roles within policing, apply to join the National Policing Fast Track Programme run by the College of Policing, or leave policing altogether. Whichever pathway they choose, Police Now is an ever-growing family for which they will be an ambassador and alumni member.

You'll be there
Visible, reliable, proud

Society needs talented neighbourhood police officers as diverse as the communities they serve. Are you ready to lead change so that even the most vulnerable can thrive?

If you want to be a leader who improves the lives of those around you, apply for Police Now's National Graduate Leadership Programme today and develop skills for life.

Join us. Change the story.
policenow.org.uk

POLICE:NOW
INFLUENCE FOR GENERATIONS

Police Now is proud that of its 562 participants on the 2020 cohort, 54% identify as female, 46% male, 17% are of black, Asian or minority ethnic heritage and 11% identify as LGBT+.

pwc.co.uk/careers

facebook.com/PwCcareersUK
linkedin.com/company/pwc-uk    twitter.com/PwC_UK_careers
instagram.com/PwC_UK_careers   youtube.com/careersPwC

Join us and find your
human difference

PwC's purpose - to build trust in society and solve important problems - is more relevant than ever. PwC's committed to helping clients and communities address current and future challenges. Join Actuarial, Audit, Consulting, Deals, Legal, Risk Assurance, Tax or Technology.

With 24,000 employees at offices UK-wide, attracting the right talent continues to be paramount. Jobs of the future will require new skills, so investing in people is central to PwC's mission and inclusive culture. Whether it's empowering their people to learn new skills for the digital world, reimagining the possible on how they work with clients, or to be open-minded on how they care for and support each other, they want to create an environment where their people can be the best they can be. This includes encouraging their teams to explore different ways of working with 'everyday flexibility', allowing a better balance of work and life, and 'dress for your day', where employees determine their work dress code.

At PwC, graduates and undergraduates can expect to be part of a stimulating environment working on challenging projects in a culture that embraces difference. Regardless of degree or background, anyone can make an impact.

PwC looks for talented graduates eager to learn, with business awareness, intellectual and cultural curiosity, and the ability to build strong relationships. Graduates develop in a supportive and nurturing learning environment - in some business areas, this could mean working towards a professional qualification. Whatever the route, hard work and accomplishments are recognised and rewarded with a competitive salary and a tailored, flexible benefits scheme.

In this new era, everyone will need to adapt and grow. It's the breadth of skills and human difference that will help people to stand apart.

Explore.
Inspire.
Reimagine.

In a rapidly changing world, we encourage you to look beyond the possible and reimagine your future. We're looking for inspired minds; whether you're designing and implementing new digital audit programmes, helping clients navigate a more complex tax world, or providing strategic consulting advice, we'll empower you to build new skills and develop ideas together.

New world, new skills.
pwc.co.uk/careers

🐦 **@pwc_uk_careers**

f **PwCCareersUK**

in **pwc-uk**

⊙ **pwc_uk_careers**

▶ **careerspwc**

Valuing Difference. Driving Inclusion.

Rolls-Royce pioneers cutting-edge technologies to sustainably meet the world's vital power needs. From building the world's most efficient large aero-engine to supporting NASA missions, Rolls-Royce transforms the potential of technology. A career at Rolls-Royce means shaping the future.

Pioneers do things differently. So, a career at Rolls-Royce means challenging the status quo and continually re-shaping the human experience. And because different ways of thinking make for better, bolder ideas, candidates will be joining a diverse, global workforce dedicated to that mission.

As these changing times have brought tough challenges for all, Rolls-Royce believes that now is the time to act as one community and one business. That includes supporting, rewarding, recognising, developing and empowering everyone in the organisation to thrive and succeed – from those who have been with Rolls-Royce for years to those who are soon to join.

For those soon-to-be-joiners there are graduate and internship opportunities for candidates from STEM and Business with STEM disciplines to join the team and build a rewarding career. It could be a career firmly rooted in collaboratively striving for the next big, technological breakthrough, or it could be a career in leadership, keeping everyone motivated, passionate and full of pioneering spirit.

People who do well at Rolls-Royce are people who are self-aware, agile, creative, innovative, bold and passionate about what Rolls-Royce does. As do people who are open-minded, collaborative and can bring fresh perspectives to enduring challenges.

A career at Rolls-Royce means learning from, and working with, brilliant minds, helping solve complex, fascinating problems and shaping the future.

GRADUATE VACANCIES IN 2021

ENGINEERING

TECHNOLOGY

NUMBER OF VACANCIES
No fixed quota

LOCATIONS OF VACANCIES

STARTING SALARY FOR 2021
£28,500

UNIVERSITY PROMOTIONS DURING 2020-2021
Please check with your university careers service for full details of Rolls-Royce's local promotions and events.

APPLICATION DEADLINE
Year-round recruitment
Early application advised.

FURTHER INFORMATION
www.Top100GraduateEmployers.com
Register now for the latest news, local promotions, work experience and graduate vacancies at Rolls-Royce.

ROLLS
ROYCE

Stand up
& Light the way

We deliver everyday power to people throughout the world
– and our focus is on making that power as low-carbon as
possible. For example, our technology has been installed
in one of Shanghai's newest buildings: the Shanghai Tower.
A compact gas-powered CHP module supplied by MTU
provides heat, power and cooling using chillers. And right
across Shanghai, MTU emergency diesel generator sets
make sure the lights never go out.

Meanwhile in the UK, we're leading a consortium to develop
an affordable power plant that generates electricity using
a small modular reactor (SMR). Our SMR technology can
produce nuclear power anywhere in the world – and with
a lower carbon footprint. It's an intelligent way to meet our
future energy needs.

We pioneer the power that matters.
careers.rolls-royce.com

Pioneers of power

ROYAL NAVY

Throughout the course of history, a life at sea has always attracted those with a taste for travel and adventure; but there are plenty of other reasons for graduates and final-year students to consider a challenging and wide-ranging career with the Royal Navy.

The Royal Navy is, first and foremost, a fighting force. Serving alongside Britain's allies in conflicts around the world, it also vitally protects UK ports, fishing grounds and merchant ships, helping to combat international smuggling, terrorism and piracy. Increasingly, its 30,000 personnel are involved in humanitarian and relief missions; situations where their skills, discipline and resourcefulness make a real difference to people's lives.

Graduates are able to join the Royal Navy as Officers – the senior leadership and management team in the various branches, which range from engineering, air and warfare to medical, the Fleet Air Arm and logistics. Starting salaries of at least £25,984 – rising to £31,232 in the first year – compare well with those in industry.

Those wanting to join the Royal Navy as an Engineer – with Marine, Weapon or Air Engineer Officer, above or below the water – could work on anything from sensitive electronics to massive gas-turbine engines and nuclear weapons. What's more, the Royal Navy can offer a secure, flexible career and the potential to extend to age 50.

The Royal Navy offers opportunities for early responsibility, career development, sport, recreation and travel which exceed any in civilian life. With its global reach and responsibilities, the Royal Navy still offers plenty of adventure and the chance to see the world, while pursuing one of the most challenging, varied and fulfilling careers available.

GRADUATE VACANCIES IN 2021
ENGINEERING
FINANCE
GENERAL MANAGEMENT
HUMAN RESOURCES
LAW
LOGISTICS
MEDIA
RESEARCH & DEVELOPMENT
TECHNOLOGY

NUMBER OF VACANCIES
No fixed quota

LOCATIONS OF VACANCIES

Vacancies also available elsewhere in the world.

STARTING SALARY FOR 2021
£25,984

UNIVERSITY PROMOTIONS DURING 2020-2021
Please check with your university careers service for full details of the Royal Navy's local promotions and events.

MINIMUM ENTRY REQUIREMENTS
Relevant degree required for some roles.

APPLICATION DEADLINE
Year-round recruitment

FURTHER INFORMATION
www.Top100GraduateEmployers.com
Register now for the latest news, local promotions, work experience and graduate vacancies at the Royal Navy.

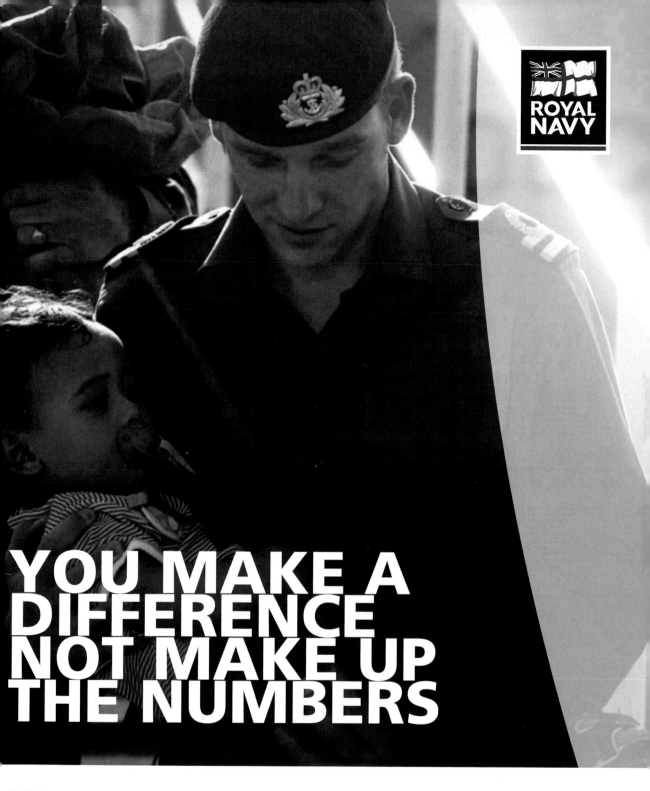

YOU MAKE A DIFFERENCE NOT MAKE UP THE NUMBERS

ROYAL NAVY OFFICER

Being an officer in the Royal Navy is a career like any other, but the circumstances and places are sometimes extraordinary. With opportunities ranging from Engineer Officer to Medical Officer, it's a responsible, challenging career that will take you further than you've been before. If you want more than just a job, join the Royal Navy and live a life without limits.

LIFE WITHOUT LIMITS
08456 07 55 55
ROYALNAVY.MOD.UK/CAREERS

savills

Savills UK is a leading global real estate service provider listed on the London Stock Exchange. The company employs over 39,000 staff and has 600 offices and associates worldwide, providing all trainees with excellent scope for international experience as their careers develop.

Savills passionately believe that their graduates are future leaders, and as such make a huge investment in them. Savills' graduates are given responsibility from day one, in teams who highly value their contribution, allowing them to be involved in some of the world's most high-profile property deals and developments. Graduates are surrounded by expert professionals and experienced team members from whom they learn and seek advice. Individual achievement is rewarded, and Savills look for bold graduates with entrepreneurial flair.

Savills are proud to have won *The Times Graduate Recruitment Award: Employer of Choice for Property* for the fourteenth year running. A great work-life balance, structured training and a dynamic working environment are amongst the factors which see Savills nominated by final year students as the preferred Property employer year-on-year.

Savills' Graduate Programme offers the chance to gain an internationally recognised professional qualification. The company offers roles within Surveying, Planning, Food & Farming and Forestry, and half of the Graduate Programme vacancies are positioned outside of London. The company has offices in exciting locations around the UK, where Fee Earners work with varied and prestigious clients. The diversity of Savills' services means that there is the flexibility to carve out a fulfilling, self-tailored career path in any location.

GRADUATE VACANCIES IN 2021
PROPERTY

NUMBER OF VACANCIES
50+ graduate jobs

LOCATIONS OF VACANCIES

STARTING SALARY FOR 2021
£23,500-£26,500
Plus a £500 sign-on bonus.

UNIVERSITY PROMOTIONS DURING 2020-2021
ABERDEEN, BATH, BIRMINGHAM, BRISTOL, CAMBRIDGE, CARDIFF, CITY, DURHAM, EDINBURGH, EXETER, GLASGOW, HERIOT-WATT, IMPERIAL COLLEGE LONDON, KING'S COLLEGE LONDON, LEEDS, LIVERPOOL, LONDON SCHOOL OF ECONOMICS, MANCHESTER, NEWCASTLE, NORTHUMBRIA, NOTTINGHAM TRENT, OXFORD, OXFORD BROOKES, READING, SHEFFIELD, SOUTHAMPTON, SURREY, UNIVERSITY COLLEGE LONDON
Please check with your university careers service for full details of Savills' local promotions and events.

APPLICATION DEADLINE
Mid-Late November

FURTHER INFORMATION
www.Top100GraduateEmployers.com
Register now for the latest news, local promotions, work experience and graduate vacancies at **Savills**.

SHAPE Y**OUR** FUTURE

"I was involved in high profile planning projects of between 2000 and 4000 homes within the first 6 months of joining Savills"

"I assisted with successfully pitching for the disposal of a portfolio of logistics assets across Northern Europe worth approximately €400 million"

"I have helped progress over 300 Megawatts of energy for the UK power grid through renewable developments - enough to power nearly 200,000 homes"

17
possible
career paths

2
year training programme
with permanent
employment contract

14
Years as The Times
Graduate Employer of
Choice for Property

40%
of our main board joined
as graduate trainees

35,000+
global employees

600+
offices in over
60 countries

A career in real estate offers an exciting and dynamic career path with the opportunity to specialise in several different areas that help shape the future of our built environment.

Become **the future of Savills**

shell.co.uk/careers

facebook.com/ShellUnitedKingdom
linkedin.com/company/shell 　 twitter.com/Shell
instagram.com/Shell 　 youtube.com/Shell

Shell is an international energy company that aims to meet the world's growing need for more, and cleaner, energy solutions in ways that are economically, environmentally and socially responsible. They are one of the world's largest independent energy companies, operating in more than 70 countries.

In the UK, Shell has been proud to play a vital role in finding and providing oil and gas for the UK for more than 120 years – helping to power industries, transport systems and homes.

The challenge for the future is to continue to meet growing global demand for energy at the same time as reducing carbon emissions. Shell is an active participant in meeting this challenge. Through collective thinking, idea sharing and learning, they are building the collaborations necessary to deliver a world with more, and cleaner, energy.

At Shell, graduates can help drive innovation forward and develop tomorrow's energy solutions today. No matter their discipline, they will have the chance to work on meaningful projects that directly impact the business, whilst receiving training and support designed to nurture rock-solid career foundations. They will have the opportunity to power their careers to new heights and to be part of a culture that changes the global energy system and shapes the future.

Roles are varied and the work ranges from developing advanced fuels and improving data processing to Human Resources and Communications. The opportunities they have are ideal for students and graduates, whose energy and passion for change can help them to achieve their goals.

Shell believes in creating an inclusive culture where their employees can thrive, so whatever a graduate's background or ambitions, they can find their future at Shell.

GRADUATE VACANCIES IN 2021

ENGINEERING
FINANCE
HUMAN RESOURCES
MARKETING
RESEARCH & DEVELOPMENT
TECHNOLOGY

NUMBER OF VACANCIES
TBC

LOCATIONS OF VACANCIES

STARTING SALARY FOR 2021
£Competitive

UNIVERSITY PROMOTIONS DURING 2020-2021
ABERDEEN, CAMBRIDGE, IMPERIAL COLLEGE LONDON, LEEDS, MANCHESTER, OXFORD, QUEEN MARY LONDON, STRATHCLYDE, UNIVERSITY COLLEGE LONDON, WARWICK
Please check with your university careers service for full details of Shell's local promotions and events.

APPLICATION DEADLINE
Varies by function

FURTHER INFORMATION
www.Top100GraduateEmployers.com
*Register now for the latest news, local promotions, work experience and graduate vacancies at **Shell**.*

THE FUTURE.
YOURS TO MAKE.

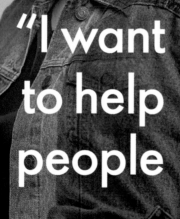

"I want to help people

My future is bringing energy to those in need"

Hayley
Engineer at Shell

Find out more at
shell.co.uk/careers

GRADUATE VACANCIES IN 2021

ENGINEERING

FINANCE

GENERAL MANAGEMENT

PURCHASING

TECHNOLOGY

NUMBER OF VACANCIES
150+ graduate jobs

LOCATIONS OF VACANCIES

STARTING SALARY FOR 2021
£28,000

UNIVERSITY PROMOTIONS DURING 2020-2021
ASTON, BIRMINGHAM, LOUGHBOROUGH, MANCHESTER, NEWCASTLE, NOTTINGHAM, SHEFFIELD, SOUTHAMPTON
Please check with your university careers service for full details of Siemens' local promotions and events.

MINIMUM ENTRY REQUIREMENTS
2.1 Degree

APPLICATION DEADLINE
Early January 2021

FURTHER INFORMATION
www.Top100GraduateEmployers.com
*Register now for the latest news, local promotions, work experience and graduate vacancies at **Siemens**.*

Siemens is everywhere you look. Building the technologies that make the world move – reinventing mobility and smart infrastructure so cities, and even entire countries, flow autonomously. Its digital visionaries, multidisciplinary engineers and business experts are forever learning.

They collaborate on innovative and prestigious projects worldwide – such as reimagining the iconic London Underground. Across the world, Siemens is building a future that's electrified, software-driven and carbon-neutral. And its influence over global infrastructure really is here, there and everywhere.

Inspired to build a truly moving future? Siemens' paid internships and graduate programmes challenge students to innovate, explore and grow day after day on real-life mentor-guided engineering projects. Its world-class programmes empower grads and interns to influence significant projects from day one. Over two years, those undergoing early careers programmes develop the technical, interpersonal and leadership skills needed to progress quickly and achieve more in their chosen career path. Siemens is looking for highly ambitious engineers and business-minded individuals studying degrees including: Software, Computer Science, Electrical & Electronic Engineering, Telecommunications, Manufacturing, Production, Automotive and Business Support.

There's a real sense of community. Together, over 100 other graduates and interns will experience Siemens' ultra progressive and diverse culture and forward-thinking approach to the workplace. Not to mention tailored programmes that reflect students' interests and all the benefits that come with it.

Ready to move beyond the theory and build a future defining a new era? The wait is over.

Heathrow

256

PICCADILLY LINE

Truly moving futures here, there and everywhere

It's time you moved beyond the theory and began engineering a smarter, more connected future.

Sky is Europe's leading entertainment company. Every day Sky makes life easier and more enjoyable for over 23 million customers across seven countries by connecting them with the best entertainment. How is this made possible? By a diverse and dedicated group of people who come from all walks of life.

Most people know Sky for its entertaining, dramatic and action-packed shows but what they may not realise is that nothing happens on-screen without the talented people behind the scenes, working their magic. The team constantly beats tight deadlines, builds the latest tech, fights digital threats and powers through brilliant projects every day.

Want to learn how to be a business leader? Develop cutting-edge products? Gain skills across the business, or become an expert in a specialist area? The range of graduate programmes at Sky gives new joiners the chance to do all this and more. They can contribute to world-renowned TV, cinema, sport, news, technology, broadband and mobile.

Sky also offers insight days and summer internships to help graduates decide on a career that suits them best. From challengers to collaborators, Sky is always on the lookout for talented and diverse graduates who want to work in a fun, fast-moving environment. The business works hard to build an inclusive culture, where everyone can be themselves. Whoever they are. Wherever they're from. Surrounded by some of the best people in the industry. Benefiting from on-the-job learning. Enjoying the opportunity to try out new ideas and shape where the business goes next. They will also get to see and do things at Sky that they simply wouldn't experience anywhere else.

So, no matter which programme a graduate decides to join, they'll be at the heart of where the real action happens at Sky.

GRADUATE VACANCIES IN 2021

CONSULTING

FINANCE

GENERAL MANAGEMENT

TECHNOLOGY

NUMBER OF VACANCIES
150+ graduate jobs

LOCATIONS OF VACANCIES

STARTING SALARY FOR 2021
£28,000-£35,000

UNIVERSITY PROMOTIONS DURING 2020-2021
BIRMINGHAM, BRISTOL, BRUNEL, EXETER, LEEDS, NOTTINGHAM, QUEEN MARY LONDON, SHEFFIELD, SUSSEX, WARWICK
Please check with your university careers service for full details of Sky's local promotions and events.

APPLICATION DEADLINE
Varies by function

FURTHER INFORMATION
www.Top100GraduateEmployers.com
Register now for the latest news, local promotions, work experience and graduate vacancies at Sky.

SLAUGHTER AND MAY/

slaughterandmay.com
trainee.recruit@slaughterandmay.com

Slaughter and May is one of the most prestigious law firms in the world. They advise on high-profile and often landmark international transactions. Their excellent and varied client list ranges from governments to entrepreneurs, from retailers to entertainment companies and from conglomerates to Premier League football clubs.

Slaughter and May have offices in London, Brussels, Hong Kong and Beijing. In other jurisdictions they prefer to remain agile by leading unified, hand-picked teams of lawyers from market-leading law firms. They are a full service law firm to corporate clients and have leading practitioners across a wide range of practice areas. The firm is committed to a forward-thinking, innovative approach to legal service delivery to complement the best in class, business-focused advice on which their reputation is built.

The firm takes great store in drawing strength from diversity. With 147 different degree courses from 70 different universities and 45 nationalities represented among their lawyers, their culture is extremely broad.

Their lawyers are not set billing targets. In this way, their lawyers are free to work collaboratively, sharing expertise and knowledge, so that they can concentrate on what matters most – the quality of the work and client service.

During the two-year training contract, trainees turn their hand to a broad range of work, taking an active role in four, five or six legal groups while sharing an office with a partner or experienced associate. All trainees spend at least two six-month seats in their market-leading corporate, commercial and financing groups. Subject to gaining some contentious experience, they choose how to spend the remaining time. They also offer open days, workshops and work experience schemes to enable applicants to gain an insight into life as a commercial lawyer.

GRADUATE VACANCIES IN 2021
LAW

NUMBER OF VACANCIES
80 graduate jobs
For training contracts starting in 2023.

LOCATIONS OF VACANCIES

STARTING SALARY FOR 2021
£45,000

UNIVERSITY PROMOTIONS DURING 2020-2021
Please check with your university careers service for full details of Slaughter and May's local promotions and events.

MINIMUM ENTRY REQUIREMENTS
2.1 Degree

APPLICATION DEADLINE
Please see website for full details.

FURTHER INFORMATION
www.Top100GraduateEmployers.com
Register now for the latest news, local promotions, work experience and graduate vacancies at Slaughter and May.

SLAUGHTER AND MAY

A WORLD OF DIFFERENCE

Laws, international markets, global institutions… all changing every day. So how do we, as an international law firm, create the agility of mind that enables us to guide some of the world's most influential organisations into the future?

By allowing bright people the freedom to grow. By training lawyers in a way that develops a closer understanding of clients through working on a wider range of transactions. By fostering an ethos of knowledge sharing, support and mutual development by promoting from within and leaving the clocks outside when it comes to billing. To learn more about how our key differences not only make a world of difference to our clients, but also to our lawyers and their careers, visit

slaughterandmay.com/careers

SLAUGHTER AND MAY/

80
training contracts

300+
workshops
and schemes

Lawyers from
70
universities

teachfirst.org.uk

facebook.com/TeachFirst f   recruitment@teachfirst.org.uk ✉
linkedin.com/company/teach-first in   twitter.com/TeachFirst 𝕐
instagram.com/TeachFirstUK ◎   youtube.com/TeachFirstUK ▶

Teach First is a charity building a fair education for all. They develop and support teachers and leaders who are determined to make a difference in the schools that need them most. Since 2002, 12,000+ talented recruits have helped change the lives of more than a million children from disadvantaged backgrounds.

Graduates have many careers options ahead of them, but few are more meaningful than teaching. Too often, the future of a disadvantaged child is determined by their postcode, not their potential – they're 18 months behind their wealthier peers when they take their GCSEs. It's clear great teachers and brilliant leaders are needed – now more than ever – to help every young person get the education they deserve.

Teach First's Training Programme is the largest teacher training and leadership programme in the UK. It offers graduates a salary while they train, real responsibility from day one and the support they need to thrive in the classroom. Over two years, they'll qualify as teachers and gain a fully-funded Postgraduate Diploma in Education and Leadership (PGDE).

Through secondary, primary or early years placements, trainees will make an instant impact on the lives of young people, in a role where no two days are the same. More than half of trainees continue teaching in schools after completing their PGDE, with many progressing quickly to leadership roles. And the charity's influential network links them to organisations who value the diverse skills they bring.

The challenge is real, but so is the chance to create lasting change. With the most important generation of teachers and leaders, Teach First is fighting for a fairer future.

Visit the Teach First website to find out more and apply now.

GRADUATE VACANCIES IN 2021
TEACHING

NUMBER OF VACANCIES
1,750 graduate jobs

LOCATIONS OF VACANCIES

STARTING SALARY FOR 2021
£Competitive

UNIVERSITY PROMOTIONS DURING 2020-2021
ABERDEEN, ASTON, BATH, BELFAST, BIRMINGHAM, BRADFORD, BRISTOL, BRUNEL, CAMBRIDGE, CARDIFF, CITY, TRINITY COLLEGE DUBLIN, UNIVERSITY COLLEGE DUBLIN, DURHAM, EDINBURGH, ESSEX, EXETER, GLASGOW, HERIOT-WATT, HULL, IMPERIAL COLLEGE LONDON, KEELE, KING'S COLLEGE LONDON, KENT, LANCASTER, LEEDS, LEICESTER, LIVERPOOL, LONDON SCHOOL OF ECONOMICS, LOUGHBOROUGH, MANCHESTER, NEWCASTLE, NORTHUMBRIA, NOTTINGHAM, NOTTINGHAM TRENT, OXFORD, OXFORD BROOKES, PLYMOUTH, QUEEN MARY LONDON, READING, ROYAL HOLLOWAY, SCHOOL OF AFRICAN STUDIES, SHEFFIELD, SOUTHAMPTON, ST ANDREWS, STRATHCLYDE, SURREY, SUSSEX, SWANSEA, UEA, UNIVERSITY COLLEGE LONDON, WARWICK, YORK
Please check with your university careers service for full details of Teach First's local promotions and events.

MINIMUM ENTRY REQUIREMENTS
2.1 Degree
However, all applications are assessed on a case-by-case basis.

APPLICATION DEADLINE
Year-round recruitment
Early application advised.

FURTHER INFORMATION
www.Top100GraduateEmployers.com
Register now for the latest news, local promotions, work experience and graduate vacancies at Teach First.

Monday morning

A. Fire up the laptop. Open Excel.

B. Fire up the classroom. Make them excel.

Learn skills that will stay with you – and your students – far beyond the classroom door. As they find their potential, you'll discover your own.

ALTER
THE
OUTCOME

T▪F Teach First

**THINK
AHEAD**

thinkahead.org

hello@thinkahead.org ✉

twitter.com/ThinkAheadMH 𝕏   facebook.com/ThinkAheadorg **f**

youtube.com/ThinkAheadMH ▶   linkedin.com/company/think-ahead-org **in**

GRADUATE VACANCIES IN 2021
SOCIAL WORK

NUMBER OF VACANCIES
160 graduate jobs

LOCATIONS OF VACANCIES

The Think Ahead programme is a new route into social work for graduates and career-changers remarkable enough to make a real difference to people with mental health problems. The paid, two-year programme combines on-the-job learning, a Masters degree and leadership training.

Mental health social workers use therapy, support, and advocacy to enable people to manage the social factors in their lives – like relationships, housing, and employment – to allow them to get well and stay well.

The Think Ahead programme focuses on adult community mental health teams, supporting people living with a wide variety of illnesses such as bipolar disorder, schizophrenia, and personality disorders. These are multi-disciplinary teams, usually within an NHS Trust, which can include social workers, nurses, support workers, occupational therapists, psychologists and psychiatrists.

Participants on the programme begin their training with an intensive six-week residential over the summer. This prepares them for frontline work by giving them a grounding in approaches to mental health social work.

Following this training, participants work within NHS mental health teams in units of four. Each unit is led by a highly experienced Consultant Social Worker, and participants share responsibility for the care of the individuals they work with. Participants become professionally qualified in the second year of the programme and are then able to work more independently.

Throughout the programme there is regular training and time allocated for academic study. The programme culminates in a Masters degree in social work. Leadership training also takes place throughout the programme, supporting participants to become excellent social workers, and to work towards leading change in the future.

STARTING SALARY FOR 2021
£19,100

UNIVERSITY PROMOTIONS DURING 2020-2021
BIRMINGHAM, CAMBRIDGE, DURHAM, ESSEX, KING'S COLLEGE LONDON, LEEDS, LIVERPOOL, MANCHESTER, OXFORD, QUEEN MARY LONDON, SHEFFIELD, SOUTHAMPTON, SUSSEX, UNIVERSITY COLLEGE LONDON, WARWICK, YORK
Please check with your university careers service for full details of Think Ahead's local promotions and events.

MINIMUM ENTRY REQUIREMENTS
2.1 Degree

APPLICATION DEADLINE
April 2021

FURTHER INFORMATION
www.Top100GraduateEmployers.com
*Register now for the latest news, local promotions, work experience and graduate vacancies at **Think Ahead**.*

THINK
AHEAD

Think Ahead has given me a deeper understanding of the impact that mental illness can have on individuals.

Jan, Edinburgh graduate
and Think Ahead participant

thinkahead.org

tpp-careers.com

facebook.com/TPPcareers **f**   careers@tpp-uk.com ✉

linkedin.com/company/the-phoenix-partnership-tpp- **in**   twitter.com/TPPcareers **y**

instagram.com/TPP_careers ◎   youtube.com/TPPsystm1 ▶

TPP is a global digital health company. With over 7,000 organisations using their solutions to care for over 50 million patients, their software is used across all health and social care settings, including GPs, emergency departments, hospitals and mental health services.

Their technology helps improve people's lives across the world, whether it is scheduling immunisations for millions of children, allowing doctors to manage complex care for elderly patients, helping governments with the prevention of outbreaks, or developing new machine learning algorithms for the early diagnosis of disease. TPP is committed to helping tackle global health challenges, working with governments to deliver the technology required for the future of healthcare.

No other company has a digital healthcare solution on this scale. Their database is one of the largest in the world. It processes a billion transactions daily – more than the London Stock Exchange and Visa combined.

TPP has been consistently recognised as an outstanding graduate employer. In both 2017 and 2018 they were awarded the "Top Company for Graduates to Work For" by the JobCrowd, and in 2020 they won the best graduate salary award! For the last two years, they have also been named in *The Times Top 100 Graduate Employers* list.

They value natural ability, enthusiasm and the potential to learn over direct work experience. As well as a great job, they will provide graduates with an excellent starting salary, fantastic benefits, and outstanding annual pay reviews.

Their offices are based in Horsforth, a vibrant suburb of Leeds. Not only does Horsforth have lots of bars, pubs and restaurants, it's also ideally placed between the city centre and the start of the Yorkshire Dales to the north.

GRADUATE VACANCIES IN 2021

MARKETING

SALES

TECHNOLOGY

NUMBER OF VACANCIES
50+ graduate jobs

LOCATIONS OF VACANCIES

STARTING SALARY FOR 2021
£28,000-£45,000

UNIVERSITY PROMOTIONS DURING 2020-2021
BATH, BIRMINGHAM, BRADFORD, BRISTOL, CAMBRIDGE, DURHAM, EDINBURGH, GLASGOW, IMPERIAL COLLEGE LONDON, KING'S COLLEGE LONDON, LANCASTER, LEEDS, LIVERPOOL, LONDON SCHOOL OF ECONOMICS, MANCHESTER, NEWCASTLE, NOTTINGHAM, OXFORD, SHEFFIELD, SOUTHAMPTON, ST ANDREWS, SURREY, SUSSEX, UNIVERSITY COLLEGE LONDON, WARWICK, YORK
Please check with your university careers service for full details of TPP's local promotions and events.

MINIMUM ENTRY REQUIREMENTS
2.1 Degree
A Level requirements (dependent on role).

APPLICATION DEADLINE
Year-round recruitment
Early application advised.

FURTHER INFORMATION
www.Top100GraduateEmployers.com
Register now for the latest news, local promotions, work experience and graduate vacancies at TPP.

SOLVE PROBLEMS. SAVE LIVES.

£45k
STARTING SALARY

Graduate Software Developer

Graduate Analyst

Marketing & Communications

Account Manager

Commercial Manager

www.tpp-careers.com

f TPP Careers 　　🐦 @TPPCareers

📷 @tpp_careers 　　in TPP

 **UBS**

ubs.com

facebook.com/UBScareers   campus-careers-emea@ubs.com
linkedin.com/company/ubs   twitter.com/UBScareers
instagram.com/UBScareers   youtube.com/UBS

UBS offers a collaborative, international and diverse working environment that rewards passion, commitment and success. They are a team of more than 66,000 colleagues, collaborating across all major financial centers in more than 50 countries speaking over 150 languages.

UBS are looking for hard-working, ambitious and highly analytical individuals to join their early careers programs, offering opportunities in Investment Banking, Asset Management and Group Functions.

UBS are offering a four-day long Spring Insights Program for students who are considering a career in banking but unsure where to start. Through a combination of workshops, interactive skills sessions, project work and networking opportunities, students will explore the possibilities at UBS whilst engaging their skills.

UBS's 10-week Summer Internship programme offers the opportunity to enhance business knowledge (and network) with business series, community days and case studies.

UBS are offering a 12-month Industrial Placement Program where students will gain invaluable experience working with a team of diverse people and enhance their skills through on-the-job training. This is a unique opportunity to learn more about UBS's culture, their people and their business.

UBS's Graduate Talent Program lasts between 18-24 months. Graduates will be directly involved in day-to-day operations, working with professionals and gaining first-hand experience of the business. As well as on-the-job learning, they will also be training on the financial markets, products and other core business topics. Rotations are a key part of some of the programs; by taking on other roles in related departments, graduates will gain a wider perspective of the bank.

GRADUATE VACANCIES IN 2021
FINANCE
HUMAN RESOURCES
INVESTMENT BANKING
MARKETING
SALES
TECHNOLOGY

NUMBER OF VACANCIES
100 graduate jobs

LOCATIONS OF VACANCIES

Vacancies also available in Europe, the USA, Asia and elsewhere in the world.

STARTING SALARY FOR 2021
£Competitive

UNIVERSITY PROMOTIONS DURING 2020-2021
ASTON, BATH, BELFAST, BIRMINGHAM, BRISTOL, CAMBRIDGE, CARDIFF, CITY, DURHAM, EDINBURGH, GLASGOW, HERIOT-WATT, IMPERIAL COLLEGE LONDON, KING'S COLLEGE LONDON, LANCASTER, LEEDS, LEICESTER, LIVERPOOL, LONDON SCHOOL OF ECONOMICS, LOUGHBOROUGH, MANCHESTER, NEWCASTLE, NOTTINGHAM, OXFORD, QUEEN MARY LONDON, SHEFFIELD, SOUTHAMPTON, ST ANDREWS, UEA, UNIVERSITY COLLEGE LONDON, WARWICK, YORK
Please check with your university careers service for full details of UBS's local promotions and events.

MINIMUM ENTRY REQUIREMENTS
2.1 Degree

APPLICATION DEADLINE
Varies by function

FURTHER INFORMATION
www.Top100GraduateEmployers.com
Register now for the latest news, local promotions, work experience and graduate vacancies at UBS.

Figuring out your future?

Let's shape it together

Ready to launch your career?

Join us on a journey and help redefine the scope of client products and services as we know them today. We have programs that are designed just for you, whatever your year of study or degree subject.

It doesn't matter if you like things fast-moving or measured. If you like fine-tuning the smallest of details or driving solutions through big data. Or if you want to enhance the status quo or invent the future. If any of this sounds like you, we want to hear from you. Come and experience our unique culture which has inclusion and collaboration at its core.

We can help you find out.
ubs.com/careers >

UBS is proud to be an equal opportunities employer. We respect and seek to empower each individual and the diverse cultures, perspectives, skills and experiences within our workforce.

Unilever

GRADUATE VACANCIES IN 2021

ENGINEERING

FINANCE

HUMAN RESOURCES

LOGISTICS

MARKETING

RESEARCH & DEVELOPMENT

SALES

TECHNOLOGY

NUMBER OF VACANCIES
30-50 graduate jobs

LOCATIONS OF VACANCIES

STARTING SALARY FOR 2021
£32,000

**UNIVERSITY PROMOTIONS
DURING 2020-2021**
*Please check with your university careers
service for full details of Unilever's local
promotions and events.*

APPLICATION DEADLINE
Varies by function

FURTHER INFORMATION
www.Top100GraduateEmployers.com
*Register now for the latest news, local
promotions, work experience and
graduate vacancies at Unilever.*

Unilever is a leading consumer goods company who make some of the world's best-loved brands: Dove, Knorr, Magnum, Lynx, Sure, Tresemmé, Simple and Hellmann's, to name a few. Over two billion consumers use their products every day. Unilever products are sold in 190 countries and they employ 155,000 globally.

Around the world, Unilever products help people look good, feel good and get more out of life. Unilever's vision is to grow its business, while decoupling its environmental footprint from growth and increasing positive social impact. Unilever is looking for talented graduates who can challenge the way things are done, bring new ideas to the table, and dare to make big decisions to help achieve this ambition.

Graduates can apply to one of the following areas: human resources, finance, supply chain, research & development, customer development, marketing, and technology management.

The Unilever Future Leaders Programme is about making a big impact on the business. It is about growing iconic, market-leading brands from the first day and tapping into continuous business mentoring, excellent training, and hands-on responsibility. Graduates will have the chance to help Unilever build a better business and a better world, whilst finding their purpose to be their best self.

Graduates will have real responsibility from day one, an opportunity of becoming a manager after three years, and a great support network to see them develop and attain their future goals. Dependant on function, Unilever will support graduates in achieving Chartered status and qualifications.

Graduates employed with Unilever have a fantastic opportunity to gain a great head start in their career, and to make a real difference to Unilever's business and the world.

CHANGE LED BY YOU

A better business.
A better world.
A better you.

JOIN NOW
unilever.com/careers/graduates

Unilever

unlockedgrads.org.uk

facebook.com/UnlockedGrads   hello@unlockedgrads.org.uk

linkedin.com/company/unlocked-graduates   twitter.com/UnlockedGrads

instagram.com/UnlockedGrads   youtube.com/UnlockedGraduates

Unlocked Graduates is a unique two-year leadership development programme that puts brilliant graduates at the heart of prison reform. Nearly half of all adult prisoners reoffend within one year of leaving prison, creating more victims, untold damage, and a cost of over £18 billion.

The problems facing prisons are some of the most complex in society. That's the challenge at the heart of the Unlocked Graduates two-year leadership development programme. Unlocked looks for ambitious graduates who are passionate about shaping the system for the better – as well as gaining a fully-funded bespoke Master's degree, a highly competitive salary, the mentorship of an experienced prison officer, unique experiences, and development opportunities with key employers.

Combining academic study with real-world experience, Unlocked provides the platform to trial and assess solutions within prisons. And in their second year, graduates get to write and present a policy paper to the Ministry of Justice.

As a prison officer, no two days are the same. Helping some of the most vulnerable and challenging people in society means being prepared for new situations – and being an advocate, negotiator, diplomat, and leader. It calls for a calm head, confidence, and problem-solving skills – all of which graduates develop with Unlocked. With real responsibility from day one, it's the rare chance to learn how to expertly face challenges head on and hone expertise in leadership and communication – whether on the prison landing or in the Governor's office.

Many graduates choose to stay within the justice system after the programme, but no matter where their career takes them, Unlocked supports a growing network of change-makers. Being a prison officer is about so much more than locking up. With Unlocked Graduates, it can really open doors.

GRADUATE VACANCIES IN 2021
PRISON OFFICER

NUMBER OF VACANCIES
150 graduate jobs

LOCATIONS OF VACANCIES

STARTING SALARY FOR 2021
£22,000-£30,000
Dependent on location.

**UNIVERSITY PROMOTIONS
DURING 2020-2021**
Please check with your university careers service for full details of Unlocked's local promotions and events.

MINIMUM ENTRY REQUIREMENTS
2.1 Degree

APPLICATION DEADLINE
Rolling deadline

FURTHER INFORMATION
www.Top100GraduateEmployers.com
Register now for the latest news, local promotions, work experience and graduate vacancies at **Unlocked***.*

vodafone

As a global tech leader, Vodafone transforms lives and businesses around the world. From developing pioneering IoT technology, to connecting 50 million unbanked people to financial services through smart phones, Vodafone connects millions of people to endless possibilities.

Vodafone's purpose is to build a digital society that enhances socio-economic progress, embraces everyone and does not come at the cost of our planet. To support this and their 670 million customers, constant innovation underpins everything Vodafone does. For example, when hit by a crisis, Vodafone takes action. Vodafone is empowering thousands of people to help the battle against COVID-19, in their sleep. The DreamLab app taps into a phone's unused processing power when charging at night, turning it into a virtual supercomputer to support vital research.

At Vodafone through real responsibility, graduates are inspired to experiment, try new things and make mistakes. After all, it's the fastest way to learn. The Discover graduate programme allows talented young minds to gain hands-on experience, technical skills, personal and professional growth and the opportunity to learn from industry experts all at a company that's an industry game changer. Graduates can make an impact in areas including Tech, Finance, Business, Commercial and HR. It's a chance to be part of a global community of graduates that are revolutionising connectivity through tech and innovation.

Vodafone relies on creatives, challengers, those that think differently, who are adaptable and thrive in a fast pace environment, to help achieve their ambitious goals. Joining Vodafone means being part of a truly diverse and inclusive group of like-minded people who want to change the world.

The Future is Exciting. Ready?

GRADUATE VACANCIES IN 2021

FINANCE
GENERAL MANAGEMENT
HUMAN RESOURCES
MARKETING
TECHNOLOGY

NUMBER OF VACANCIES
150-200 graduate jobs

LOCATIONS OF VACANCIES

STARTING SALARY FOR 2021
£33,000
For Technology roles.

£30,000
For non-Technology roles.

UNIVERSITY PROMOTIONS DURING 2020-2021
ASTON, BATH, BIRMINGHAM, LEEDS, LOUGHBOROUGH, NOTTINGHAM, QUEEN MARY LONDON, UNIVERSITY COLLEGE LONDON, WARWICK
Please check with your university careers service for full details of Vodafone's local promotions and events.

MINIMUM ENTRY REQUIREMENTS
2.2 Degree

APPLICATION DEADLINE
Varies by function

FURTHER INFORMATION
www.Top100GraduateEmployers.com
*Register now for the latest news, local promotions, work experience and graduate vacancies at **Vodafone**.*

Emergency phone signal delivered by drone. You in?

And that's just one of our revolutionary projects defining the future of tech and communications.

But we need exceptional graduates to make them happen. Join us, get hands-on experience across a huge range of specialities and be part of something extraordinary.

Discover our graduate opportunities –
careers.vodafone.com

The future is exciting.
Ready?

jobs@wellcome.ac.uk

twitter.com/WellcomeTrust facebook.com/WellcomeTrust

youtube.com/WellcomeTrust linkedin.com/company/wellcome-trust

Wellcome is a global charitable foundation, both politically and financially independent. Wellcome exists to improve health for everyone by helping great ideas to thrive. It supports researchers, takes on big health challenges, campaigns for better science, and helps everyone get involved with science and health research.

Wellcome supports transformative work, such as co-funding the development of an Ebola vaccine, campaigning to secure change in mitochondrial donation, and launching Wellcome Collection. In 2020, Wellcome is supporting global research efforts to overcome the COVID-19 pandemic.

As well as funding scientific and medical research, Wellcome works at the intersection of health and society, and so is looking for graduates from all backgrounds. For recent graduates, Wellcome offers two-year development programmes. The general programme gives experience of four different jobs for six months each. These could involve working with Wellcome's Africa and Asia Programmes, writing parliamentary briefings, or finding ways to engage the public. Wellcome also offers career-specific programmes in areas like investments for those who are ready to specialise.

Whichever programme graduates choose, they'll be valued team members, with support from mentors, line managers and peers. With a focus on development, the programmes encourage graduates to work outside of their comfort zone, to expand their potential.

At the end of the programmes many graduates go on to more senior roles at Wellcome, while others move to other charities, further study, cultural venues or even setting up their own businesses. Whatever graduates choose, Wellcome values ongoing relationships with its alumni so they can continue to make a difference in global health.

GRADUATE VACANCIES IN 2021

GENERAL MANAGEMENT
HUMAN RESOURCES
INVESTMENT BANKING
MEDIA
RESEARCH & DEVELOPMENT
TECHNOLOGY

NUMBER OF VACANCIES
12 graduate jobs

LOCATIONS OF VACANCIES

STARTING SALARY FOR 2021
£26,000

UNIVERSITY PROMOTIONS DURING 2020-2021
BATH, BRISTOL, BRUNEL, CAMBRIDGE, CITY, KING'S COLLEGE LONDON, KENT, LANCASTER, LEEDS, LEICESTER, LONDON SCHOOL OF ECONOMICS, MANCHESTER, NOTTINGHAM, QUEEN MARY LONDON, READING, ROYAL HOLLOWAY, SCHOOL OF AFRICAN STUDIES, SHEFFIELD, ST ANDREWS, UEA, UNIVERSITY COLLEGE LONDON
Please check with your university careers service for full details of Wellcome's local promotions and events.

MINIMUM ENTRY REQUIREMENTS
2.2 Degree

APPLICATION DEADLINE
Varies by function

FURTHER INFORMATION
www.Top100GraduateEmployers.com
Register now for the latest news, local promotions, work experience and graduate vacancies at Wellcome.

wellcome

"One of the best things is being part of a community of other graduates who together form a network across the whole organisation and share ideas, experiences and knowledge from beyond our own specific roles"

Poppy, 2019 graduate

WHITE & CASE

GRADUATE VACANCIES IN 2021
LAW

NUMBER OF VACANCIES
50 graduate jobs
For training contracts starting in 2023.

LOCATIONS OF VACANCIES

STARTING SALARY FOR 2021
£48,000

UNIVERSITY PROMOTIONS DURING 2020-2021
Please check with your university careers service for full details of White & Case's local promotions and events.

MINIMUM ENTRY REQUIREMENTS
2.1 Degree

APPLICATION DEADLINE
Please see website for full details.

FURTHER INFORMATION
www.Top100GraduateEmployers.com
Register now for the latest news, local promotions, work experience and graduate vacancies at White & Case.

White & Case is a global law firm of more than 2,000 lawyers worldwide. They've built an unrivalled network of 44 offices in 30 countries. That investment is the foundation for their client work in 180 countries today. Many White & Case clients are multinational organisations with complex needs that require the involvement of multiple offices.

White & Case trainees will work on fast-paced, cutting-edge cross-border projects from the outset of their career. White & Case is looking to recruit ambitious trainees who have a desire to gain hands-on practical experience from day one and a willingness to take charge of their own career. They value globally-minded citizens of the world who are eager to work across borders and cultures, and who are intrigued by solving problems within multiple legal systems.

The training contract consists of four six-month seats, one of which is guaranteed to be spent in one of their overseas offices.

They offer vacation scheme placements over the winter, spring and summer, open days and two-day insight schemes. These provide a great way to experience first-hand what life is like as a White & Case trainee as well as gain useful insight into the firm and the training they offer.

The firm's virtual learning platform offers the opportunity to gain first-hand insight into life as a White & Case trainee and experience the realities of cross-border law. There is no cost to access the platform; it is self-paced to fit around users' schedules, and no application form or legal knowledge is required. Students will gain insight into the fast-paced, cutting-edge projects their lawyers and trainees work on, and gain valuable skills by undertaking true-to-life legal tasks. Participation in the learning platform will be recognised on their application forms.

Together we make a mark

Graduate careers in law

As a trainee in our London office, you will have the opportunity to work on challenging cross-border client matters providing you with international experience and exposure from day one. Join us and make your mark.

whitecasetrainee.com

1

of the only law firms to offer a guaranteed overseas seat

75

vacation scheme places per year in London

£48k

year-one trainee starting salary

44

offices across 30 countries

50

trainees recruited per year in London

£105k

salary on qualification

WHITE & CASE

Useful Information

EMPLOYER	GRADUATE RECRUITMENT WEBSITE	EMPLOYER	GRADUATE RECRUITMENT WEBSITE
ADMIRAL	admiraljobs.co.uk	HSBC	hsbc.com/earlycareers
AIRBUS	jobs.airbus.com	IBM	ibm.biz/graduate
ALDI	aldirecruitment.co.uk/graduate	JAGUAR LAND ROVER	jaguarlandrovercareers.com
AMAZON	amazon.jobs	KPMG	kpmgcareers.co.uk
AMERICAN EXPRESS	careers.americanexpress.com/students/UK	L'ORÉAL	careers.loreal.com
ARMY	britishar.my/tt100	LIDL	lidlgraduatecareers.co.uk
ASTRAZENECA	careers.astrazeneca.com/students	LINKLATERS	careers.linklaters.com
ATKINS	careers.atkinsglobal.com/graduates	LLOYDS BANKING GROUP	lloydsbankinggrouptalent.com
BAE SYSTEMS	baesystems.com/graduates	M&S	marksandspencergrads.com
BAKER MCKENZIE	uk-graduates.bakermckenzie.com	MARS	careers.mars.com
BANK OF ENGLAND	bankofengland.co.uk/careers/early-careers	MI5	mi5.gov.uk/careers
BARCLAYS	joinus.barclays	MORGAN STANLEY	morganstanley.com/campus
BBC	bbc.co.uk/careers	MOTT MACDONALD	mottmac.com/careers/uk-and-ireland-graduate
BLACKROCK	careers.blackrock.com/students	NATWEST GROUP	jobs.natwestgroup.com
BLOOMBERG	bloomberg.com/careers	NETWORK RAIL	networkrail.co.uk/careers/early-careers
BMW	bmwgroup.jobs/uk	NEWTON	workatnewton.com
BP	bp.com/grads/uk	NGDP FOR LOCAL GOVERNMENT	local.gov.uk/ngdp
BT	bt.com/graduates	NHS	nhsgraduates.co.uk
CAPITAL ONE	jobs.capitalone.co.uk/earlycareers	PENGUIN RANDOM HOUSE	penguinrandomhousecareers.co.uk
CHARITYWORKS	charity-works.co.uk	PINSENT MASONS	graduate.pinsentmasons.com
CIVIL SERVICE	faststream.gov.uk	POLICE NOW	policenow.org.uk
CLIFFORD CHANCE	careers.cliffordchance.com/london	PWC	pwc.co.uk/careers
CMS	cmsearlytalent.com	ROLLS-ROYCE	careers.rolls-royce.com
DELOITTE	deloitte.co.uk/careers	ROYAL NAVY	royalnavy.mod.uk/careers
DEUTSCHE BANK	db.com/careers	SAVILLS	savills.co.uk/graduates
DLA PIPER	dlapipergraduates.com	SHELL	shell.co.uk/careers
DYSON	careers.dyson.com/early-careers	SIEMENS	siemens.co.uk/earlycareers
ENTERPRISE RENT-A-CAR	careers.enterprise.co.uk	SKY	skyearlycareers.com
EXXONMOBIL	careers.exxonmobil.com	SLAUGHTER AND MAY	slaughterandmay.com
EY	ey.com/uk/students	TEACH FIRST	teachfirst.org.uk
FRONTLINE	thefrontline.org.uk	THINK AHEAD	thinkahead.org
GCHQ	gchq-careers.co.uk	TPP	tpp-careers.com
GOLDMAN SACHS	goldmansachs.com/careers	UBS	ubs.com
GOOGLE	google.com/students	UNILEVER	careers.unilever.com/uk/en/uflp
GRANT THORNTON	trainees.grantthornton.co.uk	UNLOCKED	unlockedgrads.org.uk
GSK	gsk.com/en-gb/careers/future-leaders	VODAFONE	careers.vodafone.co.uk/graduates-students
HERBERT SMITH FREEHILLS	careers.herbertsmithfreehills.com/uk/grads	WELLCOME	wellcome.ac.uk/graduates
HOGAN LOVELLS	graduates.hoganlovells.com	WHITE & CASE	whitecasetrainee.com

109734